three, four, open the door

CREATIVE FUN FOR YOUNG CHILDREN

BY
SUSAN M. STEIN
AND
SARAH T. LOTTICK

FOLLETT PUBLISHING COMPANY F CHICAGO

Library of Congress Catalog Card Number: 70–161631
ISBN 0–695–80275–5 cloth binding
ISBN 0–695–80276–3 paper binding

Second printing

DEDICATED
TO
OUR CHILDREN

ADAM,
EDWARD,
NOAH,
MARGARET,
PAUL, and
KAREN

TABLE OF CONTENTS

chapter 5. fun and easy toys to make 96

chapter 6. scientific experiments 111

chapter 7. games 131

chapter 8. outdoor activities 154

preface

Several years ago we began developing a handbook of activities for small children. We had become aware of the work of Jean Piaget, Benjamin Bloom, and Jerome Bruner, showing children's learning ability to be at its peak before the age of five. These ideas and our experiences with our own children showed us that mothers have limitless opportunities to help their young children develop learning skills before they start formal schooling. Furthermore, the widespread interest in Head Start, in Montessori schools, and in traditional nursery schools indicated that parents wanted to widen their children's horizons. Concomitant refocusing of kindergartens to provide a more advanced scholastic program suggested that educators were prepared to implement the discoveries of the educational psychologists.

We also realized that increasing numbers of mothers, from choice or necessity, are pursuing careers outside the home. Child care centers that are not merely custodial but that are enriching for the child are needed more than ever, especially for the disadvantaged. Creative care is one of the high-priority goals of the Women's Liberation movement, some labor unions, employers' organizations, social service groups, and government leaders.

In addition, men are becoming more involved with young children. More men are choosing teaching as a career and many fathers have begun assuming some of the child care responsibilities that formerly were carried out almost exclusively by mothers.

Therefore, we have written this book for any adult—male or female, professional or paraprofessional, parent or teacher—who is involved in caring for and teaching young children from birth to six years of age.

As teachers and parents we have high hopes for our

children. We would like them to be mannerly, neat, and well-behaved, but not restricted or frustrated in personality development by too much attention to trivial detail. Allowed to be satisfyingly messy, yet trained in the direction of responsibility. Civilized, but not suppressed, and able to express anger without harming others. Motivated, but not goal-obsessed.

Children do not automatically acquire these virtues. They need help. But we all have our limits of patience, resourcefulness, and fortitude. No matter how hard we try, we cannot be all things to a child all of the time. We can only pick and choose our way among the theories, strive for consistency, and hope for the best. Meanwhile, we must cope with these energetic, curious, exploring personalities around us who demand to know, "What can I do now?"

Children, of course, do not always ponder what to do next. Instead, they may ricochet from one activity to another, dawn to dusk. But restlessness, bickering, or general high spirits on the part of a child can frequently alert an adult to impending chaos. We hope this book will help you respond in a calm and creative way. With minimum effort and preparation, you will be able to divert quarrelsome children, entertain lonesome ones, and, at the same time, develop their imagination, coordination, and sensory perception.

You must take two preliminary steps. First, plan the environment with the children in mind. In a home, put kitchen toys in the kitchen and quiet games in areas meant to be kept relatively presentable. Don't forget to provide at least one rough and tumble spot.

At home or school, toys should be stored on child-sized shelving units in order to develop the child's sense of responsibility and save you time and work. You can impose a rule that a toy must be returned to the shelf before a new one is taken down, but don't expect the rule to immediately or permanently assure order.

Secondly, you must have certain supplies on hand. A list in the back of the book suggests materials to start you out. Other materials are mentioned in various chapters. You can add to these suggestions as your children's interests grow.

When you are ready to try an activity in this book, read the directions until you understand the activity well and can present it in your own words. Then ask the child if he would like to do something fun. A little enthusiasm on your part helps to interest children more quickly. If you explain a project by doing, such as making a totem pole from an egg carton, discreetly remove your illustration to allow the child creative freedom and to avoid discouraging him when his project doesn't look exactly like yours.

If, after your explanation, you find that the child is not converting the egg carton into a totem pole but into a space crawler, or is not painting a picture of flowers but seems intent on depleting the supply of paints, be content that he is busy and happy. Compliment him on his effort by showing your interest in his work. Generally reserve judgments of good and bad, since what is good to you may be bad to a three year old, and since, if you are like most adults, you will tag anything good that has been produced by an endearing child. Instead ask him questions that lead him to talk with you about his work.

All the ideas in this book have been used successfully with our own preschoolers and their friends—and in some instances have actually been suggested by them. We have attempted to bypass the theoretical dilemmas. Rather, we offer practical ways for you to help preschoolers grow along a number of lines and we hope that these ideas will be useful irrespective of your theoretical preferences. Our common goal is helping children to better understand and enjoy their world and themselves. Let's help them open the door!

CHAPTER 1

to begin at the beginning

A baby learns from the moment of his birth. Between the extremes of passivity (sleeping) and powerful expression (screaming), he learns from his environment as he interacts with it. From birth on he is progressively and rapidly expanding his perception of his environment through sight, touch, taste, hearing, and smell. He seems to experiment. From feeding to feeding he perfects his nursing technique. From movement to movement he becomes more familiar with his surroundings. And from crying as a general expression of discontent, he rapidly develops specific cries to elicit specific responses from his environment.

His development of perception and discrimination depend upon the variety of stimuli to which he is exposed. If his environment remains always constant, he is less aware. Changes produce responses, and responses expand awareness. A child learns that there will be food when he is hungry, burping and cuddling when he is uncomfortable, a dry diaper when he is wet, and sleep when he is tired; that he can rely on others for the security that results from the satisfaction of these needs. And when he is physically and emotionally comfortable, he will enjoy a more stimulating existence if there is gentle variety in his life.

The more aware an adult is of an infant's early learning, the more learning opportunities he can present by such actions as imitating sounds, putting items within reach, and smiling. Smile and laugh at a baby, and one day, when he is about a month old, he will smile back. You may follow this up by experimenting to see what makes him smile and, later, laugh. Imitate his other sounds and try to stimulate him to produce them again. You will help him to discover his abilities and you are having fun together.

When a baby seems intrigued by a certain toy, present him with variations on it. If he enjoys dropping rings on a dowel, give him a set of graduated rings, first to stack on a dowel, then on each other. Next give him sets of increasingly smaller rings to thread. When his interest in rings and dowels wanes, observe what his next interest is and capitalize on it.

Remember, though, to present new experiences gradually. Besides the ideas in this chapter, many can be gleaned from the chapters that follow. Even a year-old child will enjoy dying Easter eggs. However, you must be careful not to introduce too much stimulation too rapidly. Too much noise can be confusing. Too many changes may produce frustration. Toys lose value if too many are available at once. Present one or two at a time and replace them when the baby becomes distinterested.

Playing with a baby is far different from playing with a toddler or older child. A baby probably does not even know where he leaves off and you begin! So, much of baby play will center around your helping him find out about himself in a very elementary way. He has hands; he can laugh and make someone else laugh; he can reach for and get what he wants. Play between the two of you will be fragmentary and apparently very simplistic. From this very elementary interaction, the baby's social personality will develop.

BIRTH TO THREE MONTHS

The brand new baby is very busy accomplishing the art of living, but before he is a month old he will have spare time to look about him. Give him something to see and hear.

Talk to him frequently, being warm and expressive, especially when changing his diapers, for he is then in the perfect position to watch your face.

Provide a mobile and vary it often. When the baby can reach far enough to pull it down, it can then be hung from the ceiling. You may put one on his crib, one on his carriage, and one on his playpen. Pull a hanger straight, bend the hook so that you can easily loop on a string or ribbon, and lash it to the side of the crib or playpen. Bend and adjust it so that objects hang freely and move easily, and the baby can watch it from his usual position. For a carriage mobile, thread a large needle with strong, fine string (black polyester reinforced thread is scarcely visible), push it through the top front edge of the hood, and tie it on. Tie a loop in the lower end of the string. Fasten a string to each object you hang, pass it through the loop and tie it on. Remove it by cutting that string rather than your hanging line.

Make a supply of hanging objects. Almost anything will do. Choose objects for their bright and intense colors and light-reflecting qualities. Objects light enough to move will stand out from their surroundings and be more easily visible. (Start objects in motion when you walk by.) Objects which make a slight noise are also attractive. Try tinfoil balls, balloons, gift-wrapping ribbons and bows, construction paper, wallpaper or foil gift-wrapping paper cutouts (See snowflakes, p. 43 for a three-dimensional one), plastic lids and flowers, brightly colored plastic flatware and measuring spoons, small colanders, spatulas. Glue two small pocketbook mirrors back to back with a string between them. Be careful not to hang heavy objects directly over a baby's head, and check your knots each time you add something new.

You can make more complex and elaborate mobiles (see chapter 3), but avoid the temptation to construct a permanent work of art. Make at least three and rotate them. You'll enjoy looking for new and exciting things to hang and adapting holiday decorations for the purpose.

Tie an unbreakable mirror to the outside of the baby's crib or playpen at his eye level so he can see himself.

Place an aquarium or bowl of fish near the playpen or crib so the baby can watch the fish in motion. Or you can have a bird in a cage nearby.

Put the baby, in his infant seat or playpen, near a window where he can see some action: leaves blowing in the wind, snow falling, children playing.

Hold an object such as a ball of yarn about a foot from the baby's face and move it slowly from side to side, watching to see if his eyes are following the motion. Start with a short arc and gradually extend it to a full 180 degrees. As with a mobile, use objects that will catch the baby's attention by their color and brightness. Rattles are especially good, for the sound may draw the baby's eyes to them.

Take the baby for walks in such a way that he can see the world: in a back pack for maximum freedom to observe, in a stroller, or propped up in a carriage. You can put an infant seat inside a carriage to improve the baby's view.

You can make a baby carrier to be worn in front or in back, depending on the age of the child and your own preference. You will need one yard of sturdy quilted cotton, 54" wide. Cut two main pack pieces, 14" wide × 16 1/2" long. To form the neck, cut out a semicircle (5 1/2" wide × 2 1/2" at its deepest point) in the middle of one 14" edge of both pack pieces. (See diagram.) Now cut two strips 9" long and 2" wide; fold in half lengthwise, turn under raw edges and stitch. Double to form loops and pin in place. With right sides together, loops pinned to the inside, stitch around three sides of the pack piece, triple stitching over the ends of loops. Clip corners and curves. Turn. Insert a rectangle of 1/4" foam rubber sheeting at the top. Use a running stitch to secure. Turn under the rough edge on the bottom and stitch. Cut two straps 54" long × 8" wide. Fold in half lengthwise, right sides together, and stitch long edges. Turn right side out.

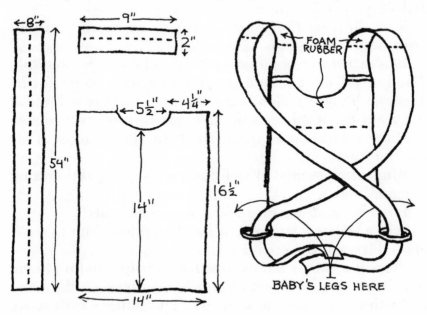

Turn in raw edges at one end and stitch. Insert rectangles of foam rubber in the shoulder areas and secure with a running stitch. Stitch across the end, catching the foam rubber, and turning in the rough ends. Pin the straps into place on the pack, overlapping the shoulder ends of the pack about two inches for extra padding on the shoulders. Stitch very securely to hold the baby's weight.

Lay the pack flat on a bed. Put the baby on it. Feed each strap through the loop on the opposite side so the straps cross. Lean over, slip head and arms through the straps, pull the straps tight and tie them in a knot behind your back, the baby held securely against your chest. Or lean backwards over the bed, slip head and arms into the straps, pull tight and tie them in front to carry the baby on your back. It is a good idea to have another adult handy to help you hold and balance the baby when you first use this on your back.

Other growth-encouraging experiences you can offer a baby:

Sing. This is the most uncritical audience you will ever have!

Play a variety of music, either radio or phonograph, but not all of the time, for there is also value in the contrast between silence and sound. Keep the volume at a reasonable level so as not to confuse or overstimulate.

Hang a windchime where the baby spends most of his waking time.

Ring a bell gently. Watch for a response and then ring it again.

Provide wind-up toys and musical animals.

When he coos, squeals, or laughs, imitate him to see if he will repeat the sound.

Press the baby's hands together to help him find them. For a few minutes a day, put red mittens on the baby with the finger sections cut off. The mittens will make him more conscious of his hands.

Place bright, easily grasped objects within his reach to encourage his handling them.

Provide him with a textured ball, book, or board. Collect a variety of materials—scraps of fake fur, plush, carpet, velvet, satin, brocade, narrow and wide-wale corduroy, seersucker, flannel, felt, wool tweed, nylon net. Choose four or five that feel the most unlike each other. To make a book, cut rectangles 4″ × 8″. Pile the pieces together. Stitch down the middle, fold on the stitching line, and top stitch ¼″ from the edge along the first stitching.

To make a texture board, use a large square of very heavy corrugated cardboard or ¼″ plywood. Glue on squares of various materials, putting contrasting textures beside each other. You can include sandpaper as one square for the board. Screw small eyes in the back of the plywood, or thread string through the corners of the cardboard and tie to the inside of the playpen where the baby can touch it. Be sure all the materials used are clean enough for the baby to put in his mouth, for he will.

Look for baby toys made from a variety of materials: hard, smooth wood; soft, fuzzy cloth; heavy objects such as a rough stone; lightweight objects of foam rubber; easily bent and twisted toys of soft rubber or cloth; and rigid toys such as plastic rattles.

THREE TO SIX MONTHS

Many of the activities introduced during the first three months will fascinate the baby for many months to come. Listening to music will inspire him to coo and sway. Watching his own face and hands in his mirror will become more exciting as he moves more and sees better. Interest in mobiles will lessen somewhat as the baby concentrates on grasping objects and putting them in his mouth, but he will still enjoy watching them as he relaxes and drops off to sleep.

Begin to play peek-a-boo. Diaper-changing time is a good opportunity.

Have one adult sit in one part of a room and another in another part. Take turns speaking so the baby will turn toward each voice.

Let older children, both friends and family, entertain the baby. Put a sheet over the side of the crib, place a strong light behind it, and have the children make shadows on it for the baby to watch. Or let them produce short puppet shows standing behind the sheet and reaching up with the puppets so that the baby sees them bobbing above his head. The sheet is not necessary, however, for the children may kneel under or by the crib and reach up to put on their show at the baby's eye level.

Tie a rattle or other small object to a string. Swing it toward the baby to within reach. If he grabs it, let him have it for a few moments before starting again.

Encourage him to grasp for smaller and smaller objects, being careful, of course, that he doesn't get the opportunity to swallow anything objectionable.

Put a raisin or a piece of dry cereal within his reach and see if he can rake it toward himself.

Put a toy out of reach and see if he will work to get it.

Try to take a toy away from him and watch him resist.

Put a block in one of his hands and see if he can transfer it to the other.

Make a response apparatus. Lay a curtain rod across the playpen so its side pieces hook down over the sides of the playpen and keep it from falling in. Tie on objects for the baby to feel: a dry and a damp sponge; a measuring cup filled with small, but not too small, objects such as plastic animals which will spill out when the cup is hit; a rattle; a spoon near a cup or two cups near each other so sound is produced when the two objects are knocked together. Look for objects interesting to touch, and objects or combinations of objects that produce noise.

Fasten a very strong elastic across the top of the playpen. Tie bracelets to it so they hang near the baby's hands. Add some small noisemakers such as jingle bells. When the baby grabs the bracelets, he will get a noise response and at the same time begin to strengthen his arm and back muscles.

Collect unbreakable containers with tight tops and in each put something that makes noise when moved: dry cereal, peas, beans, rice, corn, macaroni, pebbles, shells, rubber and metal washers. These can be fastened to either of the above two apparatuses. Or simply put a string through or around the top of a container, place the container on the floor beside the playpen or crib and place the string over the side and within the baby's reach. To make it easier for him to grasp the string, tie a clothespin onto it within reaching distance. Then tie the loose end to the bottom crossbar of the side of the playpen. When the baby pulls on the clothespin, he will raise the container off the floor, making some noise; and when he releases it, it will fall back with considerably more noise!

Hang a toy drum in a corner of the playpen near the baby's feet. He will kick it against the wooden slats to make a noise.

Crumple a newspaper or stiff wrapping paper and put it near the baby's feet. When he kicks it, the paper will rustle.

Help the baby get more reward for his hand-to-mouth movements by putting objects in his hands that will give him different sensations, and which may help relieve teething irritation. Try a clean handkerchief, small rattles, hard plastic, ivory, gold and silver bracelets, small unbreakable cups with small handles, spoons (if plastic, be sure they will not break when chewed), tongue depressors, small plastic can lids. Check all objects for points to protect against eye damage. Be sure nothing is breakable.

Cut large pieces of carrot, celery, potato, or turnip for the baby to suck on. And don't forget cookies!

When the baby starts playing with his blanket (pulling it up over his head, for instance) try a variety of materials and colors for play coverings. For example, cotton flannel or knit pajama top, quilted bathrobe, loosely woven or crocheted carriage robe, turkish towel, smooth satin comforter, or nylon negligee.

SIX TO TWELVE MONTHS

Many babies are now beginning to move about, to creep, crawl, stand, and, at about a year, perhaps to walk. The development of their own mobility engrosses many of their waking moments. They thoroughly explore their environment, investigating every nook and cranny, indoors and out. They are learning to make recognizable noises, play So Big and peek-a-boo, and wave bye-bye. They can handle objects with purpose.

Make funny noises to encourage the imitation of speech sounds.

Give the baby old magazines and newspapers to look at and tear up.

Give him cloth and cardboard books with easily recognized objects and read to him frequently, naming animals, people, and things while his attention lasts.

Let him play with an empty cup. When he is holding it fairly well, put in a teaspoonful of water. When he manages to get that much in his mouth, increase the quantity.

Put a counting frame or abacus in the playpen for hours of bead manipulation.

Collect easily grasped objects in boxes and unbreakable jars for the baby to dump and explore the contents. A large dish detergent bottle, top cut off with a knife, makes a good container for three or four clothespins. Show the baby how to drop the clothespins, one at a time, back into the bottle.

Cut a hole in the plastic lid of a coffee can, making it large enough to easily admit an object such as a block or teething bead. Show the baby how to put the block in the hole. Give him several to put in, then take off the lid for him to dump them out and start again. He will soon learn to take the lid off himself.

Put a handful of dry cereal (round or doughnut-shaped, not flakes) in a plastic dish and give it to the baby. He will eat it piece by piece, perfecting his thumb and forefinger grip. Raisins do very well if the baby can digest them.

Give him an article of clothing with an easily operated zipper, such as his sleeper or snowsuit. As he perfects his pincer grip, he will be able to work the zipper.

Give him a piece of clothing, such as his overalls, with all of the snap fasteners closed. He will soon learn to open them.

Show him how to pound two blocks together.

Give him a drum and a block, a peg pounding board and a block, and later a wooden hammer.

Put an inch or two of water in a baby bathtub or small wading pool, indoors or out, for many minutes of splashing fun. At about a year, the baby will want a cup to fill and dump.

Play catch. Sit on the floor a few feet from the baby and roll a large ball to him. Show him how to sit with his legs apart so that he can catch it.

Provide him with his own purse for carrying a few

special toys.

Place a large cardboard carton on its side where he can crawl into it. Begin to play hide and seek by pretending you can't find him anywhere. Later on, hide in a very obvious place, well within his range of vision, such as under a table, and let him crawl to you.

Place a shallow cardboard carton or large wash basin on the floor and he will enjoy crawling in and out of it and sitting in it.

Help him learn to climb downstairs. Going up is easy. Teach him to come down by turning him around so that he faces the stairs; then move his legs down one stair at a time, all the way to the bottom. You will both feel more secure if you teach him this as soon as he starts climbing up.

If he insists on climbing out of his crib or playpen, lower the side so that he has less distance to fall and show him how to get a foothold on the mattress and crossbar on the way down. If he keeps trying to climb out of an unstable high chair which will tip as he moves over the side, you will have to harness him in. But if the chair is a sturdy, bottom-heavy one, help him learn how to climb out without falling.

Put your changing table near a window or mirror, or change diapers on a bureau beside a window to keep the baby happily occupied. Talk about what you both see. Learn to change diapers on a standing baby when he is finding it impossible to lie flat on his back for more than a few seconds.

TWELVE TO TWENTY-FOUR MONTHS

The baby is becoming a toddler, acquiring greater mobility, becoming increasingly communicative, constantly investigating. He has emptied every cupboard to which he has been allowed access and will soon reach the point where he occasionally returns a thing or two to its place. He knows that wastebaskets, although very interesting, need not be dumped twice a day. He wants to help push the stroller during walks, although he is still content to ride in it some of the time. He is learning to feed himself, drink from his cup, and by the end of this period is a candidate for toilet training. In fact, during the course of this second year of life, he is developing into an independent individual with a distinct and unique personality, and a mind very much his own.

He will be telling you his wants without crying. Encourage him by vocalizing yourself. Ask, for instance, "Do you want a drink?"

Teach him different parts of the body and he will soon be able to point to at least one when it is named.

Give him verbal directions: "Put your coat on the hook."

Using a picture book, ask him to point to something, such as a bird. Read to him at least ten minutes a day.

Give him jumbo crayons and non-toxic felt-tipped pens for drawing. Teach him to draw only on paper and keep him well supplied with it.

Mix up some fingerpaints (see chapter 2) and put him in the bathtub with them. When he's finished painting, run the tub full of water to wash it and him.

Show him how to move his arm to make a puppet move. Nibble at him with the mouth of a puppet, and then have his puppet kiss you while he makes the kissing sound. (For more puppet ideas, see chapter 4.)

Pretend to feed a doll or teddy bear with a spoon and help it "drink" out of a cup. The child will copy your actions.

Have a tea party, pretending to eat and drink.

Give him a pitcher of water to pour into large cups, if you don't mind having the table, floor, and child get wet.

Otherwise, give him a pitcher of rice or dry cereal.

Include him in your housework. He will love to help you dust.

Provide him with a child-sized broom, dust mop, dust brush and pan, and let him help wipe up and sweep up after his own spills.

Provide him with laced-up shoes to unlace, and later show him how to push the shoestring through the holes.

Help him remove his own clothes. Hats are easy. With coats, you remove one arm, let him get his other arm out.

Let him help you put on his clothes. Let him try to put on his own hat, depending on the style; hold out his arms for shirts and sweaters; lie down and put up his legs for overalls and snowpants. Give him a pair of large, loose socks and mittens to practice with when he begins trying to put on his own.

When he is almost two, you may help him learn to put on his own shoes.

Help him to wash and dry his own hands.

Give him his own toothbrush to chew and teethe on.

See if he can build a tower of wooden blocks. Give him two first and show him how to put one on top of the other. Later when he can do this easily, provide him with three, then four blocks. At two years, try a tower of eight.

Give him a stack of paper or plastic cups to separate and restack.

Show him how to kick a ball forward and how to throw a ball overhand.

Find a whistle which can be blown with ease and let the child watch you blow it. Let him play with it until the noise gets to be too much for you.

Let him blow out matches.

Help him experiment in walking backwards.

Provide a wheeled vehicle he can sit on and push with his feet and toys to push and pull while he walks.

If his legs are long enough when he approaches two, provide him with a tricycle.

Help him walk upstairs and down, counting as you go. Show him how to jump in place.

Ostentatiously sniff at very strong-smelling substances, then hold them under the child's nose. If he imitates you, he will eventually get a whiff of the vanilla, cinnamon, or perfume. Smelling flowers in summer is a good substitute activity for pulling them up.

At two, the baby is becoming a child. With him, explore and enjoy the world you share. Soon, he'll be ready for the activities in the following chapters.

CHAPTER 2

paint
and
paper

From his first year on, a child enjoys color and his own manipulation of it. Painting is an exciting introduction ✳ to color, manual skill, design, and visual observation, as well as being a most intriguing enterprise.

Most of the following suggestions concern variations in technique and material. For the most part, children enjoy being given free rein. At certain ages, particularly around five, children also find very structured activities satisfying and like working on a specific object.

Don't forget that most two and three year olds still have a rather short attention span. For your own convenience, set up the painting equipment so that it is easily accessible. Keep basic paints, brushes, paper, smocks, and table covering or newspaper together so that setting up and cleaning up can be done quickly when children want to paint. A particularly good time for daily painting at home is right after a meal, when the table can be cleared, set up for painting, and the children are busy and in sight during the dishwashing.

When you demonstrate any technique, especially when your greater skill is obvious, get your example out of sight. Preferably, throw it away. Children are quick to realize that their work suffers by comparison with an adult's.

Some specific suggestions: Dry tempera is the best long-term investment. It can be mixed with water as needed, and can also be mixed with detergent, liquid starch, and salad or baby oil and used to create a great variety of effects. Liquid tempera is more expensive and dries up rapidly. Water colors are standard equipment, but the colors are not intense enough for young children, the hard cakes are difficult to soften for quick painting, and they easily become muddy. Crayons are also standard equipment, and children will use them frequently, but they are not nearly so exciting as paint. Felt-tipped pens and markers are useful and fun to have on hand.

Use egg cartons or muffin tins to mix small amounts of dry tempera. Get large brushes which hold a lot of paint—stiffer bristles for younger children. Help keep colors bright by changing the rinse water often. Better yet, provide a brush for each color. Except for special techniques, use newsprint, which is very cheap and comes in large sheets.

For paper cutting, a child needs a pair of scissors that cuts easily. For safety's sake, they should be blunt, and the rule of not carrying them from place to place, but leaving them at the work area, is of major importance. For a left-handed child, get left-handed scissors when he is two years old. All good stationers and school supply stores sell them. Newsprint, in colors as well as white, provides a cheap paper supply. Don't forget old magazines, cut for color rather than the objects pictured in them, and old newspapers, paper sacks, and discarded gift wrapping.

For collage, white glue is easiest; homemade paste is cheapest. A very easy recipe for paste is given on page 39. This paste has the advantage of being so cheap that you can let the children use as much as they like. To simplify cleanup, cover the table with newspaper.

When children first start to make collages, they usually paste one piece of paper on top of the next, the finished product being a pile of very well-pasted paper. If you manage to tolerate this, you will find that by the third attempt the child has begun to see the possibilities of design on his own. A two and a half year old will be satisfied with two or three objects pasted in place. A four year old will paste great quantities and enjoy watching the design grow as he adds to it. A five year old will work toward a preconceived design, using fewer materials, but each with purpose. When children are first starting collage work, limit the choices to ten or twenty ready-to-paste pieces or things, so that they are not overwhelmed by too complex a task. Later they will enjoy picking and choosing from a large box of miscellaneous materials.

LINE DRAWINGS AND CRAYONING

Window and mirror drawings. Let the child try to outline what he sees in a mirror or through a window with a washable felt-tipped marker. Have him try to do this with one continuous line and on a variety of surfaces, such as a toaster or coffee pot which reflects a distorted image.

Hidden-picture puzzle. A child can make a hidden-picture puzzle for a friend to solve. First he draws something recognizable or traces shapes on a paper. Then, using the same pencil or crayon, he scribbles all over the paper, disguising the original picture.

Picture books. Even though a child may not be able to

write, he can tell stories. Have him dictate one to you and then let him provide illustrations for it. The difficult part of this activity for an adult is restraining his impulse to correct the child's grammar, sequence of events, and so on. Simply record what he says.

Scrap paper trees. Show the child how to draw tree trunks with a crayon, starting at the roots and drawing the line up to the branches. Make a number of lines from the roots up to the branches so the drawn tree grows in the direction that real trees grow. He may then add a number of leaves by drawing them or by tearing a piece of green (or in the fall, yellow, red, or brown) paper into tiny scraps and gluing them on.

Duplicating. This is very simple, but seems like magic to a child. Simply staple a sheet of carbon paper between two sheets of plain paper. Lines drawn on the top sheet will, of course, appear on the bottom sheet. Variation: Put some flat object, such as a piece of cardboard cut in an interesting shape, between the top sheet and the carbon paper. Rub the top sheet hard with the back of a spoon or the edge of a tongue depressor. The carbon will transfer the shape to the bottom sheet of paper.

Drawing in the dark. Give a child, sitting at a table with his paper on some newspaper, a felt-tipped marker or crayon, and ask him to draw with his eyes shut or with a blindfold on. Perhaps you will want to challenge him by suggesting he draw specific objects (square, circle, house, tree), and see what a surprise his picture is when he looks at his drawing.

Totem poles. Using the bottom of an egg carton, the child draws an eye on each egg cup. There will be six pairs of eyes. Let the child decide whether he will make both eyes in a pair alike or different. The finished totem pole can be stapled to a piece of paper and posted on a bulletin board or fastened with magnetic holders to a refrigerator door.

Life-size portraits. Have the child lie down on a large piece of brown paper and trace around him. He will be thrilled to see his shape and will enjoy coloring in details, such as features and clothes. (These portraits make nice remembrances for relatives or friends who live far away.)

Fabric design. Using permanent felt-tipped markers, a child can make a design on a placemat, napkin, bib, apron, paint smock, or even a dress. You may want to experiment with the washable kind, which bleaches out in one wash, and comes out by itself in three. Use the strong part of old sheeting for bibs (line with plastic), aprons, and smocks. Buy unbleached muslin for a dress, placemats, and napkins. A cotton knit T-shirt can also be decorated in this way, but is harder to draw on, being stretchy. In general, draw the pattern of the object on the large piece of uncut material with a pencil or colored chalk. Lay it flat on a hard surface and keep it as taut as possible by holding the edges with heavy books or thumbtacks. After the material has been painted, cut out the pattern, and finish any sewing that needs to be done.

The designing may be done with crayons instead of markers. Iron the material to melt the wax into the fibers. (Protect the ironing board and iron with paper or old cloths.) Crayon designs will also survive several washings.

TRACING, STENCILING, AND PRINTING

Tracing. Find objects with interesting shapes and textures such as coins, pieces of screening, onion bags, burlap, corrugated cardboard, scraps of cardboard arranged in a design. Or carry your paper with you and hold it over brocade upholstery, embossed book covers, lightly carved furniture, mesh covering on amplifiers, stucco walls, mosaic floor coverings. Outdoors, try tree bark, rocks, bricks, gravestones, and house numbers. The technique is simple. Hold a sheet of paper over the object to be traced. Try not to let it move. Then rub it with the flat side of a crayon or the side of a pencil point and watch the design appear on the paper.

Notched crayons. Make designs with crayons on paper by rubbing with the sides, rather than the ends of the crayons. To make the design more complex, cut notches in the sides of the crayons. These may be evenly spaced, or irregular, large notches, small ones, or just slits or chips. Show the child how different colors may be rubbed over each other, or at angles, to get plaid and checked effects.

Stencils. Stencils can be approached in two ways. Decide on a simple design such as a butterfly, draw it on a piece of heavy paper or cardboard and carefully cut it out so you have two pieces: the butterfly shape and the frame into which it fits. For the first technique, simply place the frame over a piece of paper and let the child fill the space with color. Or place the shape on a piece of paper and have the child rub a piece of colored chalk or a crayon sideways across the shape and onto the paper. The child can use heavy paint brushed on with a wide stiff brush, or he can blot paint on with a piece of sponge or a wad of damp paper towel.

Children enjoy simply tracing around shapes with a pencil or crayon. Whereas three year olds will see each shape as a unit, fours and fives will arrange a series of shapes in a pattern, and enjoy combining shapes to make pictures. Basic shapes which lend themselves to many designs are a circle, triangle, square, rectangle, and oval. You might make a supply of each of these from heavy cardboard to become part of your standard painting equipment.

Stamp pad printing. Buy a stamp pad at the dime store. Or make one by cutting four to eight pieces of old, soft absorbent cloth to about 3″ × 5″ and laying them in a pile on a small plate or in a box lid. Pour ink over the cloth until it is just barely saturated.

You can print with almost anything. Children who are just learning their letters will have a lot of fun with an alphabet set, but it is not at all necessary. You can print with a nail head, a screw, a nut, a coin, a paperclip. Small pieces of wood and art erasers, carved or not, make interesting designs. So does a piece of sponge cut into shapes or left as is. Modeling dough and clay can be molded into interesting shapes, dried, and used to print with. Make designs with crosscut sections of green pepper, onion, carrot, turnip, and celery; or use a wire or plastic hair roller, vegetable brush, bottle brush, or toothbrush.

Children love to make finger and hand prints and, of course, foot prints.

Potato prints. Cut a potato in half. Make a design in the cut surface. You can do this by drawing a simple design with a pencil (fish, flower) and cutting the potato away from the outline. Or cut the shape out leaving a potato frame. A child can make a design with a fork, spoon, or table knife by gouging and cutting notches in the cut surface.

Brush the cut surface with a thick mixture of tempera and water, and stamp the design on paper. Repeat the print, lighter and darker in color, or in a combination of colors, overlapping, scattered at random, or carefully arranged. Paper printed in this way can be used for wrapping paper, book covers, box covers, and so on, as well as just being enjoyed for its own sake. Plain paper towels can be printed as bibs for small visitors to use.

Transfer prints. Paint an object, such as a leaf or fern with thick paint. Place it painted side up on a piece of scrap paper or newspaper. Place a clean piece of paper over the leaf and rub it with a spoon. Pull off the top paper (and the leaf if it sticks).

Crayon transfer. Color the veined side of a leaf or other interesting object with crayons, using several colors if desired. Put newspapers on the ironing board. Put a sheet of paper on the board; lay the leaf, colored side down, on the paper. Cover it with another sheet of paper and press with a warm iron for a few seconds. Remove the cover paper and leaf.

Crayon painting. Grate old crayons over a sheet of wax paper, or shave them with a potato peeler. Place the sheet carefully on a newspaper-covered ironing board. Place another sheet of wax paper on top, and iron gently with a warm iron.

Or, carefully arrange gratings of crayon on a piece of glossy white shelf paper, lay on ironing board, cover with another piece of shelf paper, and iron with a warm iron. Pull the sheets apart for two crayon paintings.

Both these techniques are satisfying as is, or they may be used to produce background paper for silhouettes or collage.

PAINTING

Fingerpainting requires a washable surface, glossy paper, a convenient water supply, and suitable paint. Covering the floor or table top with newspaper eliminates a lot of wiping up. If children roll up their sleeves and wear a painting smock, or undress down to their underwear, you minimize fussing.

Make a paint smock from a man's discarded shirt. Rip off or cut off the collar, cut the sleeves off between the child's elbow and wrist. (If you are going to hem the sleeves and insert elastic at the wrist, cut them longer to allow for the hem.) Cut off the bottom of the shirt at about the knees. Put it on the child with the opening at the back and fasten it with a safety pin, sewn-on ties, a button (using the buttonhole in the neckband), or a hook and eye.

You can use fingerpaint paper, sold at art supply stores. You can also use ordinary white shelf paper, which is much less expensive. Actually, children can fingerpaint on any kind of paper, but since the paper has to be wet, most kinds fall apart. Also, as a result of wetting the paper, paintings dry with a great many wrinkles in them. Those you want to preserve may be pressed on the back with a warm iron. (Cover the ironing board with newspaper.)

Children can also paint directly on a linoleum or plastic table top, in the sink or bathtub on the enamel, or on a piece of oilcloth. To preserve a picture painted on these surfaces, smooth a paper over the painting and carefully lift it off.

The children may wet their own paper if you supply them with a bowl of water and a large sponge. Or you may wet the paper for them by dipping it quickly in a dishpan of water, or running it quickly under a faucet. Show the children how to put a dab of paint on the wet paper and spread it around so that the entire paper is covered. They will quickly discover that they can make many designs on this surface with their fingers, nails, knuckles, palms, fists, arms, and elbows. They can make lines, dots, and broad strokes by pushing, pounding, squiggling, and scratching. Let them help themselves to more paint of different colors but keep your supply of individual colors clear by using wooden or plastic spoons for each color. Let the children explore the qualities of paint themselves. Most early paintings will be brown when finished, for children find the process of mixing the colors together much more fascinating than the color of the finished product.

Recipe for easy fingerpaint: Mix dry tempera with liquid starch to the consistency of thick cream. Mix in soap flakes if desired to help thicken paint. Variation: Rub liquid starch over the paper after wetting it. Set out an egg carton filled with several colors of dry tempera. Let the children mix the dry tempera with the liquid starch on the paper as they work.

Traditional recipe for fingerpaint:

Mix 1 cup dry starch
      1 cup cold water

Pour this mixture into 2 quarts of boiling water and boil for five minutes.

Add 2 cups soap flakes
      1 tsp. glycerine

Cool, divide into small jars, color each jar with wet or

dry tempera. (Food coloring can be used, but it is rather pale.)

Painting variations.

Make a thick mixture of tempera and water and glob it on cardboard to give a highly textured effect.

Mix tempera with egg white and thin with a little water. This dries to a beautiful shine.

Mix tempera with liquid detergent to paint on water resistant surfaces, such as plastic cartons, cellophane.

In addition to painting with brushes, try the following:

—Dip the edge of a piece of cardboard in paint; use it as a brush. Cut notches in it to vary the effect.

—Paint with feathers or cotton-tipped sticks.

—Roll paint on with a cardboard roll, moving the roller in different directions.

—Wrap cloth around a finger to use as a brush.

—Dip string or yarn (the thicker and more absorbent the better) in paint and drag it across the paper.

—Wrap string on a finger or on a stick (hard twine works best for this).

—Fold paper in half. Open. Arrange saturated string on one half. Fold other half over and press.

Translucent painting. After painting picture with water color or tempera, paint over it with salad oil. Hang it in the window for the light to shine through.

Confetti painting. Sprinkle homemade confetti (scraps of construction paper, magazine pages, etc.) on a wet finger painting.

Multicolored background. Paint a sheet of paper in blocks of water color. Run some areas into others and let dry. Draw over this backing with a fine brush and black tempera, or a black crayon.

Etching with paint. Using crayons, color a sheet of paper with many different colors, pressing down hard. Mix black tempera with a little detergent. Cover the crayoned sheet with this paint until no color shows and let it dry. To etch a picture, scratch away the black paint, using pins, nails, Popsicle sticks, or fork tines, so that the varied colors below will show through in an interesting design.

Rubber cement resist. On paper, draw a design (thick and broad) with rubber cement. When it is dry, paint over it with tempera, or use the marbelized painting method described next. When the paint is dry, peel off the rubber cement. (If it hasn't been put on thick enough, you'll have to rub it off, which may smear the paint.) The space initially covered with rubber cement will be white.

Marbelized painting. Fill a large shallow pan half full of water. Drop a small amount of oil base paint into the water. Or make a thin mixture of tempera and salad oil and drop some on. Gently blow on the water to create a design. Drop the paper on the water and pick it up quickly. Let it dry.

Wax resist. Draw a picture with a white or yellow wax crayon or with a leftover birthday candle on white paper. Paint over the paper with black tempera or black water color. The crayon design will show through. (This is a good technique for ghostly Halloween pictures.)

Blot painting. Put a blob of thin paint in the middle of a piece of paper. Fold and open the paper to see the design created. Use several colors and watch them blend. Or blow on a puddle of thin paint and watch it take shape.

Chalk painting. Make a thin syrup from sugar and water, and cool. Dip a piece of colored chalk in the syrup and apply it to paper. The child may then spread the color around with his fingers or a brush.

Chalk on wet sheeting. Wet a square of sheeting and wring it out. Let the child draw a picture on it with colored chalk. When wet, the colors will be dark and thick; when dry, they will be pastel and will not smear. You can do the same thing on paper. Wet heavy brown paper (from paper sacks) with a sponge. Draw on it with chalk. Working with the side of the chalk produces interesting effects.

Detergent pictures. Mix one-fourth cup of powdered dish detergent with two tablespoons of water and beat until creamy. With this mixture the child fills in an outline drawn on cardboard or heavy paper. He may add buttons for eyes and other such details while it is wet. Suggested shapes are a snowman or a rabbit.

Painting with what's around. You can mix food coloring with hand lotion, cold cream, baby oil, and so on, to get a variety of interesting effects. You can also paint with mustard, catsup, mayonnaise, peanut butter, and jam. Obviously, the paintings cannot be preserved indefinitely.

Painting on windows. Mix water with about a one-fourth cup of cleansing powder until it is the consistency of cream. You may use this white, or add a small amount of tempera. Pastel colors are best since they admit light. Paint on windows with fingers or brushes.

Cellophane on window. Tape a large piece of colored cellophane to a window. Paint it with black tempera mixed with liquid detergent (one-fourth cup of tempera to about two tablespoons of detergent)—a very thick mixture. Use small brushes. You can also tape up tissue paper and paint on it with felt-tipped markers.

Blindfold painting. Let children paint blindfolded to see what effects they get. This works especially well with paint mixed with detergent or liquid starch on colored or brown paper.

Spatter painting. For directions see chapter 9, Greeting Cards.

COLLAGE

Scrap paper collage. Save all the bits of construction

paper and other interesting paper from other activities. These may be pasted on a backing paper of construction paper or cardboard, or may be cut or torn to other shapes. Paper may be arranged in an overlay design, or edges may be carefully fitted together to achieve a mosaic effect.

Before being glued on to the backing paper, construction paper may be glued or stapled into tubes, curled with the sharp edge of a blade of a pair of scissors, cut into fringes, folded into various shapes and the folded edges glued in place or wadded into small or larger balls. These techniques provide a 3-D effect.

Recipe for homemade paste:
    Mix 1 cup flour
          1 cup cold water
    Pour this mixture into
          3 cups boiling water, stirring constantly
    Boil gently until the mixture is clear
    Add 1 tsp. powdered alum as a preservative
    Keep in a tightly covered jar.
    If you plan to store pasted materials, add 1 tsp. powdered cloves or red pepper.

Tissue paper collage. Cut or tear various colors of tissue paper into different sizes and shapes. Dilute white glue half and half with water. Brush glue onto a sheet of newspaper or newsprint and place the tissue paper on top, overlapping the tissue pieces until the entire area is covered. Spray the dried work with hair spray or shellac to bring out the full depth of the tissue overlay.

Sticker collage. Very small children love to lick. Give them leftover Christmas stickers and the commercial advertising stickers that come in the mail. Let them stick as many as they like on a small sheet of paper. The result is almost always attractive.

Colored sand, salt, sawdust, or rice. Rub a small amount of sand with the side of a stick of colored chalk. Spread it in a box top and arrange shells on it. Or fill a small glass jar with layers of varicolored sand. Or spread glue on a piece of cardboard and sprinkle colored sand thickly on the glued areas. Use different colors.

You may get a similar effect by using either salt or sawdust which has been shaken in a jar with some dry tempera for coloring, or rice which has been shaken with a few drops of food coloring.

Colored popcorn pictures. Buy a bag of colored popcorn. Use the unpopped corn, sorted into piles of different colors, to compose a mosaic picture. Spread glue for one color area on cardboard and cover with kernels of the appropriate color. Continue to add patches of color. Finish by putting extra glue on any loose kernels.

Shell pictures. Break shells into pieces of various sizes. Glue them on cardboard to form a design. Make interesting pictures by using shells in combination with sand, small stones, and small shells.

Crepe paper pictures. Make a number of small wads of colored crepe paper. Paste these to a cardboard backing to form a design. Combine this with painted or crayoned details, or fill the whole cardboard with wads. The latter is rather ambitious for a young child.

Toothpick pictures. On a backing of colored construction paper, the child makes lines of clear drying glue. He then makes his design with wooden toothpicks. The toothpicks may be used whole, or broken into varying lengths to approximate curves, or add details. To assure success, use airplane glue and flat wooden toothpicks.

Yarn pictures. Let the child dribble a picture with white glue on heavy paper, and then lay pieces of yarn over the glue. This is most interesting when there is a choice of sizes and colors of yarn.

Cardboard pictures. Use cardboard backing. Glue cardboard pieces to it, gluing them on top of each other to varying thicknesses, in order to get a relief effect. When the glue is dry, paint the whole thing one color. This technique gives a professional result even for a three year old.

Cellophane pictures. Collect bits of cellophane from package wrappings, or buy some at an art supply store or a gift wrapping counter. Using a white backing paper, overlay the different colors to get a multicolored effect. If you have the primary colors, you can use them to demonstrate very vividly the combinations which make the secondary colors.

See and feel pictures. Give the child a variety of materials to work with—old pieces of sponge, buttons, sandpaper, foil, rick-rack, cotton balls and so on. He may glue these on heavy paper, and when finished, close his eyes and try to identify the different items by feel.

Silhouettes. Cut silhouettes from black or dark colored paper. These may be profiles of people, of course, drawn by placing a strong light directly behind a person's side view and drawing around the shadow cast on a paper taped to the wall. But for small children, simple silhouettes of dogs, trees, flowers, or abstract shapes, or lacy paper doilies cut from dark paper will be more within the range of their ability.

These may be mounted on background paper decorated by fingerpainting, or watercoloring, scraps of paper mounted as mosaics, or on tissue or cellophane which has been glued to a cardboard or construction paper frame.

PAPER CUTTING

Calico cats. Cut animal shapes from wallpaper samples. The pattern of the wallpaper makes these a lot of fun, and making up new animals and strange creatures from outer space is an exciting variation.

Spirals. Starting at the center of a piece of paper, draw a spiral round and round out to the edge of the paper. Trim off the corners so the outer edge is more or less a circle. The child starts cutting at the point where the spiral reaches the outer edge, and follows the line into the center. This is fun to do for its own sake, and also produces an interesting decoration for a mobile.

Paper doilies. Fold a paper in quarters, then cut in from the folded edges, and cut zigzags or scallops around the unfolded edge. Be sure to leave connecting pieces along the folded edges. Unfold to see the design. You can also fold the paper in half to make designs that are symmetrical left and right, but not top and bottom.

If the paper is folded back and forth several times, and cut in from each folded side, up from the bottom, and down from the top, carefully leaving connecting pieces along the folded edges, the result will be a chain of the same design or object. You may show children how to make chains of boys and girls in this way, leaving the hands and skirts as the connecting pieces of the girls, or the hands and the corners of the trousers as the connecting pieces of the boys. And, of course, bunnies, hearts, flowers, and so on can be cut so that they form a chain. You will need to outline the cutting lines with a pencil for a child to cut these out himself, whereas he can do abstract designs with little or no direction.

Snowflakes. Cutout snowflakes are distinguished from doilies by being folded into six parts so that the resultant snowflakes are hexagonal, as are real ones. First, fold the paper in half. Mark the midpoint of the folded edge. Then fold each half of the folded edge toward the other and overlap them so that the folded paper is divided into thirds. Trim the protruding corners along the shortest edges of the folded sides. If this is done correctly, and you open up your paper to check it, you will find you have a six-sided figure. Cut triangles, arcs, points and so on into all the folded edges, and into the cut edges, being sure to leave pieces of the folded edges intact as the connecting pieces.

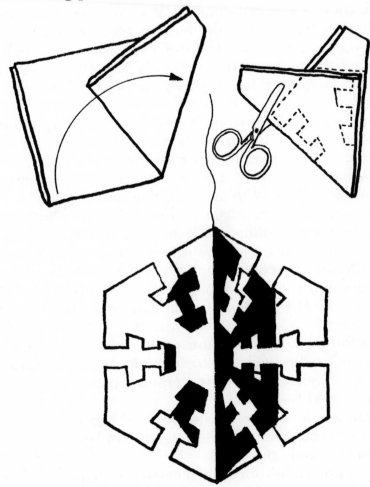

3-D Snowflakes. Cut two snowflakes at the same time as directed above, so that they are identical. Do not cut off the center point. When the design is completed, unfold the snowflakes carefully, then fold each one in half from one of the six points to the opposite point. Lay one snowflake, folded in half, on top of the other so that the folds of each are together. Staple them together three or four times as close to the folded edges as you can. Fold the top layer back, turn over and fold the bottom layer back. Attach a piece of string at the same time that you staple these top and bottom layers together at the top. Staple them together at the bottom, too. These folds at the center of the snowflake form a stiff core which helps it keep its shape as it sways in the air. Hang by the string. Foil gift wrapping is especially successful for making these.

Holey doilies. Fold paper in any way: halves, quarters, sixths, or eighths. Using a hole puncher, punch as many holes as you can at random or in a design. Unfold.

The most interesting of these cutouts may be mounted on contrasting paper to make very beautiful pictures.

Paper chains. Make paper chains by cutting strips of paper $1/2''$ to $1 1/2''$ wide and $6''$ to $9''$ long. Whatever size you choose, make the strips uniform for the best effect. If the children can work a stapler, use that. Otherwise, use glue. Show them how to make a circle of one strip, then insert the end of the next strip in that before fastening it in a circle.

In addition to construction paper, magazine paper of the better quality makes colorful and interesting chains. You can also use heavy gift wrapping paper, especially the embossed foil kind.

Filigree chain. Before fastening the strips of paper together to make the chain, punch a number of holes in them with a hole puncher.

Shaping up. Give your child a variety of shapes cut from colored construction paper, magazine pages, newsprint or whatever. The child will probably want to help cut these out. Let him construct a picture such as a house from a square and a triangle or a tree from a rectangle and a circle. If he wishes, discuss the shapes with him, letting him feel the differences.

It's a puzzle. A simple picture from a magazine can be glued on heavy paper and cut into five pieces or more, depending on the child's age. Greeting cards also make good puzzles and needn't be mounted.

Braids. Children will enjoy learning to braid. Tie three pieces of yarn, rope, twine, lanyard strips, or twisted strips of crepe paper to a door knob. Show them how to fold the outside string over the center one, first left, then right, to make a braid. Help the child tie a knot in the end. This is fun by itself, and may also be useful for a collage, doll's hair, animal's tail, lasso, or gift wrapping tie.

CHAPTER 3

modeling and construction

Three-dimensional structures are very satisfying to the creator. Working with malleable materials seems to fulfill some of our deepest, most instinctive needs. Using building materials of different varieties, the child develops the muscles of his hands and arms, some skill in working with materials and tools, gradually establishes the criteria by which he judges the success of his work, and acquires far greater understanding of the work of others. The child who has made clay sculptures and pots of his own sees a Cretan pot 3,000 years old as an object linked to his own experience and appreciates the skilled artisan who designed and decorated it. And when he sees a house being built, he is aware that it is happening by the same process he has used to build boats and wooden animals.

MODELING DOUGH

Modeling dough is a substitute for clay. It is much easier to work with any of the following kinds of modeling dough than with plasticene, the other major clay substitute, particularly for a small child whose hands are not strong enough to work plasticene when it is "cold" and whose attention span is not long enough to allow for long periods of warming up any substance. Modeling dough does not make truly permanent objects, as does clay, but it is a wonderful toy, and special creations can be preserved fairly well by baking or drying, as described below.

You can buy modeling dough, or make it from one of the following recipes. Each kind has its own special qualities, and you may want to try them all.

Commercial modeling dough is the easiest and by far the most expensive. If kept well covered—use a plastic sandwich bag inside the box it comes in—it lasts pretty well.

Least expensive is the following recipe, which lasts just as long, if not longer, when kept in a tightly closed plastic bag, and you can color it to suit yourself. It is easily handled by small children and is ideal for play.

Modeling dough made with flour:
    Mix   2 ¼ cups flour
          1   cup salt
    Add   1   cup water mixed with
          2   Tbsp. vegetable oil
Color the dough in either of the following ways: Add food coloring to the water and oil before mixing them with the dry ingredients. Or add about ¼ cup of dry tempera to the dry ingredients for a very bright dough. You'll have to cut the flour by about 3 tablespoons or add about ¼ cup more water. The dough must be kneaded or worked for a bit to become elastic. If it still seems too dry

after kneading, add water a tablespoonful at a time. It gets gooey if too wet but if it does, just add more flour. On a humid summer day, add more flour and keep it in a plastic bag in the refrigerator.

For rapid drying, bake this dough in an oven at 200° or 250° for one to two hours. The length of time needed for baking will depend on the size of the pieces. Or dry objects at room temperature for two or three days or more, again depending on their size and on the humidity. When fully dry, objects can be painted and shellacked.

Modeling dough made with cornstarch:

    Mix   1   cup cornstarch
            2   cups baking soda or salt
    Add 1 1/4 cups cold water
                  food coloring, if desired

Mix food coloring with water before adding to dry ingredients. Cook over low heat, stirring constantly, until very thick. Cover and cool. When this is cool enough to handle, work or knead it until it is elastic and easily workable. If it starts to dry out while you are using it, wet your hands to smooth it and make it pliable again. Use water to seal the seams.

The advantage of baking soda over salt is that it is finer and less grainy. Objects made from salt reflect light somewhat, however. You may want to experiment with both to see which you prefer. This dough molds beautifully and takes impressions very well. Objects made from it dry pure white or true color at room temperature in a few days. It may be baked at 200° for an hour or two but turns brownish and air bubbles may distort the shape. This dough is particularly good for making permanent objects.

Working with modeling dough. It is a very important measure of self-defense to establish rules and regulations for modeling dough the very first time it is presented, and to enforce these rigorously. As long as a certain area is carefully designated as the only place in which dough is allowed, cleaning up will mean only wiping the table and sweeping the floor.

Modeling dough can be anything the child wants it to be. To encourage self-expression, give the child a lump, take one yourself, and pat, roll, fold, and knead it. The less said about the objects formed by this action, the less confined the child is by the need to make a recognizable thing, and the greater his pleasure in the malleability of the substance itself. As the child learns, by experience, the nature of modeling dough, it becomes an extension of his imagination, and perhaps even a form of communication. When the child has become accustomed to working with modeling dough, and is using it to express his own ideas rather than depending upon yours, he is ready for you to suggest more specific ideas.

Modeling dough as dough. Modeling dough is wonderful for pretend kitchen play. All ordinary kitchen utensils can be used; dull table knives, muffin tins, gelatin molds, and rolling pins are especially good. Toy utensils are not necessary, but can add to the fun, and doll dishes make it possible to serve the cake one has just baked. You can extend the game by using a cardboard carton for a stove, and another for a refrigerator. Make these as elaborate as you like, cut an oven door, and make burners on the stove with a felt-tipped pen. Put shoe boxes inside the refrigerator carton for a freezing compartment and hydrators.

Modeling dough objects as toys. If you are careful not to put too much emphasis on the necessity of a realistic appearance, a child will be free to call any lump of dough anything he likes. Once the lump is labeled, it can be part of any game that develops around it. You can suggest a very specific game, such as Old MacDonald's Farm, and sing the song with the child. He can make the animal appropriate to each verse from a lump of dough and move it into the barnyard. You can play games centering on zoos and circuses, as well as farms, with these animals, and games about people and places with lumps of dough as friends, neighbors, teachers, aunts, uncles, cousins, grandparents, and, of course, parents and siblings. Storybook and cartoon characters can come to life, too. Larger lumps can be designated as places and things. You may have trouble keeping all these lumps identified, but the child won't.

Modeling dough makes a very good load for a miniature dump truck, and a good construction site for small bulldozers and loaders, passengers for boats, hazards for raceways, and roadbeds themselves.

Modeling dough can be made into a variety of permanent objects. The flour dough can be used for this, but the cornstarch variety, since it dries so beautifully and is less brittle when dry, is better. It's best to dry things slowly at room temperature, but small or thin objects made of flour dough can be baked with only minor discoloration. A large lumpy object may crack somewhat as it dries without necessarily detracting from the finished product. Any object that is dry can be painted, either with watercolors for a delicate effect or with tempera for a bright and bold effect. Objects can be shellacked, sprayed with a plastic spray, or coated with clear nail polish. They are not waterproof, but are otherwise quite sturdy.

Four and five year olds will enjoy mastering the pinchpot, coil, and slab techniques. Help when necessary, but try to let the child carry through on his own.

Pinchpot. Use the pinchpot technique to make small bowls. Pat a large lump into a ball, press your thumb into the center and pinch around the sides, gently and evenly, to form the desired shape. A simple candle holder is made by patting the dough into a ball, and gently pressing a candle into it. Use enough dough to make it stable. Remove the candle to let it dry. Using a large lump of dough, you may make a holder for an extra large candle, or a holder for several small tapers. You may make a long, rather narrow holder for a row of candles. These may be textured, and after drying, painted and shellacked. Bright orange dough makes a handsome jack o'lantern candleholder for Halloween. Or use green dough to make a small advent wreath for birthday-size candles at Christmas.

Coil. Form a long coil by rolling dough against a hard surface with the flat of both hands. Starting at one end, coil it into a circle the size of the bottom of a bowl. Then build up the wall. Moisten the edges of the coil to seal it together. If the dough begins to dry, wet your hands with water as you work. You may leave the coil design intact, or smooth it out with water.

When using either pinchpot or coil techniques, aim for a uniform thickness of the wall. You cannot build dough up very high unless you let the lower areas dry enough first to support the weight.

Slabs. A slab is simply dough patted out flat, or rolled with a rolling pin. Modeling dough slabs lend themselves best to cutouts. You can use cookie cutters, or a table knife, to cut out any shape you can think of. A slab may be used to form the bottom of a bowl or basket, and additional dough pinched on to the edges to build up the sides. If you let a slab harden long enough to hold its shape, you may be able to use it to form straight sides. Dampen the edges to be joined so that they hold together. A child's success with this technique of joining vertical slabs to a flat base depends on the texture of the dough (cornstarch is better than flour for this purpose) and on its degree of wetness—dry enough to hold its shape, damp enough to join completely. If he would like to try it, start with an object, such as a coaster, with very low sides. Concentrate on doing a good job of joining. He may then try an object with sides an inch or so high. When a child becomes really interested in careful building with dough, it is time to move on to clay.

Texturing. Poking anything into modeling dough to make its surface more interesting counts as texturing. Any utensil (knives, forks, spoons) or hardware (paper clips, nails) can be used to make a design which will add to the interest of the finished product. Children enjoy experimenting with various textures to form patterns and designs, whether or not they are constructing an object.

CLAY

Working with clay is very similar to working with modeling dough. Clay, however, is more rewarding even for the smallest child, for several reasons. It is more pleasant to handle. It retains forms better as it dries. More techniques are possible, and all techniques work better.

Buy wet rather than dry clay which you must mix yourself. It is ready for use, and therefore worth the small difference in cost. If you are new to clay, you will also avoid dealing with the difficulties of deciding whether or not it is damp enough, seasoned enough, and so on. You may buy clay at hobby shops, art supply stores and through established ceramic shops or ceramic teachers, or, frequently, through organizations like the YMCA or YWCA or city-run recreational centers where pottery is taught.

For having fun making small pieces, where their survival in the kiln is relatively unimportant, you needn't worry too much about wedging. The object of wedging is to eliminate air bubbles, which will weaken a piece and may cause it to explode in the firing. First, see if the clay needs wedging. Many clays sold commercially do not require it. Cut a lump of clay in half with a knife. Examine the cut edges. Only if there are several good sized air bubbles do you need to work on it.

There are two methods of wedging. The first is to slam the air out of the clay by throwing it with force against a hard surface, that is, the floor or table top. Do this several times, then cut the clay again to see if the bubbles have been eliminated. The second method is to work the clay with the hands to force the air out. This process is the reverse of kneading bread. Push down and back on a lump of clay with one hand while turning it with the other hand, pushing the particles of clay together and forcing the air out.

Drying should be done slowly. Ideally, one would use a damp box, or any cupboard where the moisture in the clay will evaporate very slowly, totally free of drafts. A good substitute for a damp box is a plastic bag, carefully wrapped around a completed object. After several days, allow some air to circulate around the object by punching a few holes in the bag. Then open the bag, turning the object inside it so that it dries evenly. When the piece is almost dry, remove the bag completely. An object is completely dry and ready to fire when it is no longer cold to the touch.

When you are setting up to work on clay, cover your table with newspapers, or, much better, with an oil cloth, bottom side up. Work over a floor which can be swept easily, for crumbs and lumps of clay are sure to fall. Provide a small dish of water and a small sponge. Actually, you will need very little water, except for final smoothing. Slip, a mixture of clay and water, whose consistency varies from potter to potter, is used for joining pieces, but is not essential to these first experiences.

Give each child a lump of clay to handle. The children may experiment with making balls, cubes, or columns.

They may try piling small balls together in different arrangements to make a variety of forms. Or they can make a cube; then cut a smaller cube from its corner and experiment with placing it at different angles on the larger cube. Experiment with grouping a number of columns of different heights in different patterns.

Two and three year olds will enjoy pinching and hand forming pieces, building by pinching on additional lumps of clay. Fours and fives do very well at this, and will also be able to join pieces successfully by scratching the edges of each, smoothing on some slip, and pressing them firmly together. If pieces are to be fired, check jointures to make sure they are firm, but be very careful not to interfere with the child's form.

Demonstrate the decorative possibilities. On slabs of clay patted flat on the table, experiment with some varieties of texturing. Get out some kitchen utensils and desk supplies: bottle opener, teaspoon, fork, melon baller, pencil, rubber erasers, and so on. Show how each can make one or more patterns in the clay. Show how repeated patterning can be effective, and how designs may be carefully arranged or result from random texturing.

As you and the children work with the clay you will discover that pinching is easiest with rather damp clay; that it is easiest to cut precisely and join clightly drier clay; that careful smoothing is best done on leather hard clay (clay that is hard enough to hold its shape but is still damp). Texturing is easiest for children on clay that is still soft.

After you have dried you pieces, you must find a kiln in which to have them fired. All of the sources of clay mentioned above are also sources of information about kilns. Most ceramists are willing to fire pieces at minimal cost. These same ceramists, as well as hobby shops, sell glazes. If the pieces the children have made are sculptural rather than utilitarian, they will not care, at first, whether or not objects are glazed. But since earthenware is still porous after firing, an earthenware cup cannot be used unless it is glazed. Furthermore, glazes are very exciting, another new adventure.

Buy the glazes that are designed for use with the clay you have, that is, will fire to maturity at the same temperature as the clay. You can rely on the ceramist for this. After objects have been bisque fired, apply a glaze to them in one of the following ways.

Dipping: This requires a large quantity of glaze, but is very easy. Simply dip the object in the glaze, lift it out, let it dry, touch up the finger marks with a little glaze on the tip of your finger.

Pouring: Prop the object over a dish or pan on two parallel sticks. Pour the glaze into it; pour the excess quickly back into the jar. Turn the object over, and pour the glaze over it again, covering it completely. Let it dry.

Touch up any spots you have missed. Pour the excess from the dish back into the jar.

Brushing: Use a brush about an inch wide and very thick. Dip it in the glaze. Do not rub off any excess. Flow the glaze onto the object as lightly as you can. Be very careful not to drag glaze with the brush, for it will not cover well if you do. Brush on three coats for complete coverage.

Clean the glaze off the bottoms of all pieces, unless you make special arrangements to have them propped up while being fired. First scrape off the dry glaze, then rub the bottom with a damp cloth.

BASIC BUILDING TECHNIQUES

Pinchpot. Hold a lump of clay in your left hand. Using the thumb and fingers of your right hand, turn and pinch gently, shaping as you go. You may add on more clay, pinching it in place. It's fun to make unusual, free-form shapes by this method. Try to keep the walls about even in thickness.

Coil. Roll out long coils of clay, using your palms and fingers, against the table top. Press the coil round and round to form a circular base, then build up the walls, shaping as you go. You can leave the coil pattern, or smooth the sides. If the clay begins to dry as you work, use slip and score the edges to get a good join.

Slab. Use a rolling pin, a large dowel, or a pipe to roll out clay as you would pie dough, using sticks or lathes about 1/4″ thick as guides for your roller to maintain uniform thickness. Let the clay dry a while so that it is stiff enough to maintain its shape. Cut out a base (circle, oval, kidney-shape), and cut a long strip of the slab (start with a rather narrow one, 1″ to 3″ wide, for easier handling). Score the edge of the base and the edge of the slab, smooth slip over both, and join them carefully. Reinforce by dabbing soft clay over the join on the inside.

Molds. Any nicely formed object can be a mold. To use a household object, such as a plastic salad bowl (do not use a good wooden one for the damp clay may damage it), cover it with two or three layers of damp cheesecloth or strips of damp newspaper or paper towel. Roll out a slab of clay. When it can be handled, gently lay it over the mold (you may use either the inside or the outside). Do not let it dry completely. As soon as it is dry enough to hold its shape (three to eight hours, depending on its thickness and the size of the object), remove it from the mold, wrap it in plastic, and let it slowly dry the rest of the way. Excellent molds are made from plaster of paris, but the process is somewhat complex. For directions, check one of the books on pottery in the bibliography.

SIMPLE ANIMAL SCULPTURES

Column. Roll a thick coil or column of clay, just three or four times as long as its diameter. Stand it on one end. Form the head and neck by pinching it in about one-third of the distance from the top to the bottom. Pinch the ears up from the top, form the nose by careful pressing and pinching, and using fingers or a tool, incise eyes and mouth. From the lower section pinch the outline of the legs, lying against the body. You may add a tail, or form one by pinching. Rather than strive for a precisely realistic effect, remember that clay lends itself best to line and form, and try to achieve a general impression of the character of the animal.

Coil. Roll two coils of equal length. Pinch them together in the middle, spreading the four ends apart. This will form the body and four legs. Add another short coil at one end, and bend it to form the neck and head. Pinch the head to form the nose and ears, and incise other features. Add a tail at the other end.

Slab. Draw the outline of a side view of an animal on paper and cut it out. Roll out a slab of clay. Cut two slabs from around the paper pattern. When the clay is hard enough to handle, lift up each animal cutout, lightly mold its curves, then pinch the two pieces together, either here and there, or all the way around. Score edges and use slip if the clay is too dry to hold well without it. You may leave this as it is, or smooth the corners and incise detailed features when it is leather hard.

Working with clay is fun, but it may also be discouraging. Have a child master simple techniques before trying more complex ones. Remember that with familiarity and practice, skill will develop and, as with most children's art work, the process is more interesting and exciting than the finished product.

PAPIER MACHE

Recipe for flour and water paste for papier mache:

Mix 1 cup flour
     1 cup water

Pour into 5 cups boiling water, stirring constantly until the mixture thickens and clears. This is a very thin paste. It will thicken somewhat as it cools.

You may also use wallpaper paste in a thin solution or a mixture of white glue mixed with an equal amount of water for successful papier mache work.

Quick papier mache. This is a simple and very successful way of making small forms. The children can make forms this way by themselves, or you may make forms for them to paint later. This is a particularly good way to make puppet heads. For details, see chapter 4.

Spread thinned glue or paste over a sheet of newspaper until it is damp. You may use a large brush or the palm of your hand. Crush, bend, fold, and twist the paper to give it its form. If starting with no object in mind, an idea may come from the paper as it is shaped. Or an interesting shape may take on a specific character when it is painted. Several sheets of paper may be used, whole or torn. When one sheet is added to another, be sure to use a lot of paste to hold them together. Let the object dry completely. Paint it with tempera and, if desired, shellac.

Papier mache sculpture. Any large papier mache figure requires an armature, that is, a frame to which the papier mache can be attached and which will support it. A frame can be made from narrow strips of wood, or of any strong wire. The most easily available material is wire clothes hangers, bendable into myriad forms.

You can make an armature for an animal from two hangers. Hold one by each end, hook up, and bend it so that it is V-shaped, with the hook still intact. Do the same to the other. You now have four legs. Bend the hook on one hanger forward, straightening it out somewhat, and hook it up and around the neck of the other hanger. This forms the back. Bend the hook of the front hanger around so that it faces forward. This hook is the support for the head.

Stuff wads of dry newspaper between the wires of each of the legs. Crumple papers, and tie them around the back and neck.

Mix up the paste recipe at the beginning of the chapter. Wet a half sheet of newspaper with the paste, crumple it up, and form it into the general shape of the head and ears, pasting it in place around the hook and onto the neck.

Tear a pile of newspapers into strips lengthwise, about one inch wide. Dip each strip in the paste and wrap it around the body, arms, legs, and head until it is completely wrapped and smooth. Give the ears and the nose their character while you do this. Strengthen the bond of the head to the neck by cross wrapping the head, extending the strips down the neck, and wrapping more strips around these and the neck, anchoring them.

You may stop here and let the sculpture dry. Or you may wrap a layer of paper toweling strips over the newspaper to give a more interesting texture when painted.

You may also wrap the sculpture in tissue paper of one or several colors, dipping the strips of tissue in paste and wrapping them just like the newspaper. This creates a brilliant color when finished and eliminates painting. Eyes and other features may be cut from construction paper and glued on.

When the sculpture is dry, and if you have not wrapped it in tissue, paint it with tempera in one or many colors. Shellac it if desired.

Papier mache pulp. Heat a large pan of hot water to

boiling. Tear several sheets of newspaper into strips, then into small pieces, 1″ × 1″ or so. Put them in the boiling water to cover and stir them around. (You might just put them to soak overnight in hot water, but boiling them speeds up the process considerably.) Turn off the fire and let the mass cool enough to handle. Squeeze out the excess water, and shred the pulp between your fingers. Add to the pulp until it is of modeling consistency: Flour and water paste, laundry starch (either cooked or liquid), or dry wallpaper paste.

This papier mache pulp may be modeled into a variety of small free standing shapes, or may be used with an armature to form large objects. You may make a basic form of crumpled and tied newspapers and cover them with the pulp. It will make excellent puppet heads. When it is dry, it may be sanded smooth with sandpaper, painted, and shellacked.

Crepe paper clay. Cut crepe paper (about one package of folded paper) into very small pieces. Place in a bowl and cover with water. Soak until soft and pliable. Drain off the excess water. Mix 1 tablespoon of salt and 1 cup of flour and add to the paper and water. If needed, add more flour to make a stiff dough. Mix well, then knead until well blended.

This clay may be molded over a bowl or ashtray. When it is dry enough to hold its shape, ease off the mold, let dry completely, and shellac.

Make beads by pinching off little bits of clay and rolling them in your hands. These may be strung when they are dry.

Pat the clay onto cans of any size and shape. Large juice cans can be small wastebaskets, soup cans make pencil holders, peanut cans with plastic lids can be penny banks (cut a slit for coins in the plastic lid), and large coffee cans with plastic lids can be cookie cans.

You can, of course, mold the clay into any form you

like, animals and people included. It can also be used to cover armatures, and to add color and texture to papier mache sculptures.

Sawdust clay. Make a thick flour and water paste by mixing 1 cup of flour and 1 cup of cold water. Pour it into two cups of boiling water, stirring constantly until the mixture boils and turns clear. Or mix wallpaper paste and water to a thick consistency.

Add sawdust to the paste until the mixture forms a dough. Work it until it handles well. This dough can be used in each of the ways listed above for crepe paper clay. In addition, because of its appearance of wood, it makes good-looking little houses and log cabins. You can also wad damp newspapers into interesting shapes and cover them with this dough. They may be painted when dry, and shellacked, or simply varnished or shellacked.

You can sometimes get sawdust in small quantities for the asking at lumberyards.

PLASTER OF PARIS

Plaster of paris may be purchased at a hardware store or building supply store, as well as at most hobby shops. Mix one volume plaster of paris to about one volume of water to a very thick creamy consistency. Put the water in the container first, then pour in the powder, in order to avoid unmixed lumps of plaster. It hardens very quickly, so mix just before using.

Plaster of paris will block drains. If you mix it in disposable containers, such as milk cartons and coffee cans, you eliminate a washing up problem. Rinse hands under an outside spigot, or in a basin of water, and throw the water away outside. Cover the work area with news-paper.

You can buy rubber molds for making small poured

plaster figures at hobby shops and school supply stores, either in sets or individually. Follow the directions that come with the molds. These figurines may be painted with watercolors or tempera, and shellacked, if desired.

Plaster plaques. Grease an aluminum pie tin (it may be the disposable type) with petroleum jelly. Place buttons and beads, seashells, pebbles, broken colored glass, and so on, in the bottom of the pan, secured by the jelly. Mix about 3 cups plaster of paris into 3 cups water to make a thick 8″ plaque or a somewhat thinner 9″ plaque. Pour slowly and carefully into the pie pan so the design is not disturbed. Insert a loop of wire, a wire hairpin, or a paper clip into the top for hanging. Let the plaque dry and remove it from the tin.

Plain plaques made the same way may be painted with watercolors or tempera. Illustrations cut from magazines may be placed face down in the pan. They will form the design when the plaque is lifted out.

Plaster may be poured into an empty pan, greased with petroleum jelly, and smoothed out. The child may then carefully grease his hand with jelly, and place it in the damp plaster, leaving the imprint of his hand to harden. Use a glue-on hanger on the back or tape on a loop of string.

Sand casting. Use a shoe box or other similar box. Put in a layer of damp sand about 2″ thick and press a design in the sand. Mix plaster and water, about three cups of each, and pour it carefully over the sand. Insert a wire hanger, hairpin, or paper clip in the wet plaster. After it dries, remove it from the box and brush off any sand that adheres. You may, as in the plaster plaques, add bits and pieces of stones, old costume jewelry, yarn and string, old coins, and other objects to the sand design so that they will be imbedded in the plaster cast. The plaster may be painted after it dries.

Plaster scenes. You can set the scene for a game of

make-believe or make a three-dimensional illustration for a story. Plaster—mounded, pushed with a stick, or carefully smoothed—forms the base.

For the setting you may use a flat area, such as a shoe box lid, or a box with the lid removed, resting on one side. The former is easier to work with; the latter has the advantage of allowing things to be hung from the top by strings to make the picture more complete.

Collect what will be needed to make the scene: twigs for trees, ice cream sticks for the walls of a fort, stones for boulders, plastic figures of cowboys, Indians, astronauts, animals, or cars. Broken toys or leftover pieces of old games might be used. A ball that has lost its bounce can be hung as a planet or cut in half to form two igloos. Remember that these things may often be painted along with the plaster to improve their appearance.

Mix the plaster and water; pour it quickly into the lid or onto the bottom (formerly the side) of the box. Quickly work it with a pencil or stick to smooth it off, push it up into hills, or make it jagged. Place your collected objects, pressing them a quarter of an inch into the plaster so they will be firm.

When the plaster dries, paint in grass, roads, and dirt. Paint the back (once the bottom), sides and top of the box to look like the sky. Hang any airplanes, birds, planets, or other sky creatures by string or thread, using a heavy needle to push the thread through the top of the box. Make a large knot to hold each in place.

Plaster and wire sculpture. Start with a block of wood, wire, nails, and bits of screening (window screen, chicken wire, quarter- or half-inch mesh, or whatever you can find).

First hammer one or more nails into the wood block. Attach the wire and let the child coil, bend, or twist it into any interesting shape or form. Fasten small pieces of screen to the wire to give the shape more bulk. The child may thread wire through the screen as you work, or tie the screen in place with very fine wire. When the child is satisfied with the form, give him a small quantity of mixed plaster and water (about one-half cup of each). Let him drip this over the wire form. He may simply let it fall where it will, adhering at random. Or he may pat it into place, building it up in particular areas. The plaster must be added rather quickly, before it starts to harden.

You may vary this technique by dipping pieces of wire to be incorporated in the sculpture in a liquid plastic or by dribbling liquid plastic over the wire form. Chunks of styrofoam may be melted with a match while held over a wire form with large tweezers and allowed to drip and adhere to the wire.

Easy sculpturing material. Mix plaster and water in a disposable milk carton. Make a cube about $2^1/_2''$ square in a two-quart carton by mixing about 1 cup water with 1 cup of plaster and adding 1 cup or more of vermiculite. As soon as the mixture hardens, peel away the carton and let the children chip away with knives or spoons. Or you may pour the mixture into a small shoe box lid (4″ × 7″) to make a relief plaque. Vermiculite comes in chunks in a variety of sizes. Building supply stores carry it in large flakes for insulation. Garden supply stores, nurseries, and hardware stores sell it in smaller quantities and tinier flakes for adding to soil.

Ice sculpture. Freeze water in a milk carton and peel off the carton. To sculpt, have the child use his hammer and screwdriver. A good activity on a hot summer day.

Styrofoam sculpture. Scraps of styrofoam from packing may be shaped by young children with dull knives, and gouged, broken, and pinched away to form fascinating shapes. Use a wooden match to melt them into a variety of drips and globs.

Soap sculpture. Carving an entire cake of soap into a shape such as a boat is a big undertaking for a preschooler. You can bring this type of project more within the reach of a four year old by giving him a small cake of soap or by softening a larger piece in water, then drying it out a bit. If it is soft enough he can gouge it as well as cut it. This is a good opportunity for establishing the rules for using a knife, the most important being to always cut away from yourself. The child will enjoy giving his sculpture different textures by using utensils such as a meat tenderizer. He can also be shown how to polish a sculpture smooth by rubbing.

Aluminum foil sculpture. A sheet of aluminum foil can be pinched, twisted, bent, and crumpled into a variety of shapes. This activity is especially nice for two and three year olds, although fours and fives, with a much more sophisticated approach, will also enjoy it.

Incidentally, because foil objects will float they make good bathtub and wading pool toys. To the children the foil may become fish, turtles, frogs, and boats.

Hammer and nails. Most children enjoy hammering nails into boards. Use scraps of wood (frequently given away by lumber yards and by workmen at building sites), common nails, and a tack hammer until the child is strong enough to handle a big one. Children may want to position the nails in a design. A four year old can build a boat by nailing a short board to a long one. A five year old can build a simple house or construct an animal from miscellaneous scraps. Since children of this age cannot yet handle a saw efficiently, they are happiest with small pieces of wood. If they are working with long boards, you will have to help them with the sawing.

Wire sculpture. Wire may be shaped with fingers into any variety of forms. Long pipe cleaners in a variety of colors lend themselves to simple and dramatic shapes. They can be very abstract or realistic. For a slightly more sophisticated technique, use a spool of medium-fine copper wire or florist's wire and a pair of pliers. Shapes may be made freely by bending and twisting or by wrapping the wire around another form, such as a pencil, and sliding it off to get a uniform spiral.

Make a star or a flower by positioning nails in a block of wood at what will be the points of the design. Pound in the nails far enough to be secure. Put a nail at the center. Wind wire around the center nail, then out to each point. Leave a piece of wire to form the stem of a flower, and end with another piece to twist around it. Carefully lift the wire off the nails.

Wire forms may be suspended from thread or supported in a lump of clay or plasticene.

STABILES AND MOBILES

A stabile is a collection of miscellaneous items supported from a base. A mobile is a collection of items suspended so that they move with the slightest motion of the air. It is much easier for children to construct stabiles by themselves since the balancing and knot-tying required for a mobile can be tedious. But children can contribute a great deal to the construction of very beautiful mobiles.

The list of materials which may be used for stabiles or mobiles is practically endless: beads, buttons, sequins, macaroni, cereals with built-in holes, straws, nuts, and washers are especially good for first attempts at stabile construction. In addition, you might try: paper, cardboard, plastic lids from coffee cans, margarine, or cottage cheese containers, Ping-Pong balls, corks, toothpicks, pipe cleaners, wire, nylon net, cellophane, aluminum foil, styrofoam, paper clips, and small broken or leftover toys.

Stabile construction. Make a large ball of clay, plasticene, or modeling dough. Let the clay or dough dry until it is solid enough to support one or more uprights. Or use half a ball of styrofoam or a large potato with one side sliced off so it has a flat base. For supports use one or more metal or wooden dowels, small tree branches of interesting shapes, a hanger pulled out to form a circle with the hook straightened and stuck in the base, pipe-cleaners, pieces of medium or heavy wire twisted, bent or coiled, straws, Popsicle sticks, cotton swabs, and toothpicks. A piece of medium or heavy wire may be laid across a wooden block, stapled in place, and the wire then bent up and shaped. Several wires may be used on one base to form a more complex structure.

Objects may be attached to these supports in any way. The youngest children will enjoy just pushing objects onto the supports, for example, threading on a pile of circle-shaped cereal. Objects may also be fastened on with twists of wire. Plastic-coated wire fasteners (the kind that are used to tie up plastic bags) are very useful for this purpose, and colorful too. Objects may be clipped to the supports with paper clips, tied on with string, or glued on with quick-drying glue.

A good beginner's stabile may be made by a child as follows: Present the child with a lump of plasticene, a number of toothpicks, and a variety of pre-cut pieces of construction paper. The child sticks the toothpicks in the lump, and arranges the paper on the toothpicks. This helps him to get the idea of arranging the form from the materials, and he may follow this up with suggestions of his own or be ready to try a variety of materials.

Mobile construction. A mobile may be made from a stabile simply by suspending the objects attached to it in such a way that they move. The tumbleweed tree described in the chapter on holidays is a mobile of this sort. However, mobiles are most often thought of as suspended from above. They may be hung from light fixtures, from cup hooks, and occasionally from curtain rods, although the proximity of the rod to the window will inhibit their motion.

Wire hangers cut with wire clippers to a variety of lengths are the most convenient supports for home use. These may be used straight or bent into arcs. Wooden dowels in a variety of thicknesses may be purchased from a hardware store and cut into any length. Toothpicks, pipecleaners, and straws are other very useful and handy supports. A circular support may be made by stapling a strip of cardboard in a circle and hanging it by three or four threads or wires. The best hanging material is size 8 buttonhole thread. Finer thread may be used, or string, or fine wire.

Start by tying up your longest support on a long thread where you can reach it easily for working. You can shorten the thread later, and move it to a better location. Tie on and balance the subsidiary supports. Then add the decorative materials.

Cosmic mobile. Use a strip of cardboard stapled in a circle for the main support. Hang it by three or four threads. Make the sun, moon, and planets by rolling up balls of aluminum foil. Thread a needle and run a length of thread through each ball in order to hang it. Or cut two circles of yellow construction paper for the sun, two of blue-green for the earth, two of red for Mars, and so on. Cut a slit in each circle from a dot in the center to the edge. Slide each pair of circles together to make a three-dimensional figure. Secure the circles with some glue along each slit, and lay the end of a piece of thread in the glue so that they will be ready to hang when dry.

To hang a moon for the earth, make a smaller cardboard-strip circle, suspend it from the larger one, and hang the earth on one side, the moon on the other. Or hang the earth from the large circle, hang the small circle by three threads so that it encircles the thread suspending the earth, and hang the moon from one side of it. Tape a small weight on the inside of the small cardboard circle to balance the weight of the moon on the opposite side.

Holiday mobiles. Shape a hanger into the appropriate shape for the holiday: heart for Valentine's Day, tree for Christmas, rabbit for Easter (see chapter 9 for a more complex version), shamrock for St. Patrick's Day. From the hanger, suspend construction paper cutouts such as hearts or jack o'lanterns or lightweight objects appropriate to the holiday such as mistletoe, pine cones, and holly at Christmas, hollow eggs at Easter.

Stained glass mobile. To make a mobile that is truly beautiful, buy liquid plastic from a hobby shop. These plastics are designed for making artificial flowers. Have children twist wire into any variety of loop or spiral shapes, leaving one long wire. Dip the loop into the plastic, stick the long wire into a chunk of styrofoam till dry, then dip the loop into a strengthener or hardener, and dry again. Use the wires to attach the plastic shapes to each other and/or to the mobile support. Or form the wire ends into small loops and hang by thread to the support.

Toothpick mobile. A young child can do most of the construction of this mobile by himself. Tie some round toothpicks together at the middle with thread, leaving two to four inches of thread between each one. Leave a long thread at one end for hanging.

The child then cuts a number of shapes (simple ones such as triangles, squares, or rectangles, or more squiggly and complex shapes) from construction paper or from a slightly pliable plastic such as lids of coffee cans and margarine tubs, all shapes being approximately the same size and weight. Using an extra toothpick, he punches a hole in each of the shapes, then pushes it onto one of the toothpicks that have been tied together.

When all the toothpicks have been decorated, hang the structure. Balance each toothpick by pushing it a tiny bit through the thread wrapped around it in the direction of the heavy end.

This structure may be made more complex by sticking a second toothpick in the decorative paper or plastic and attaching more paper or plastic to the other end of that toothpick. Two toothpicks can be made to move as a unit by sticking them both in a single piece of paper or plastic.

Toothpick structures. These may be hung as mobiles or stuck in a base to make stabiles. Spread out newspaper. Assemble flat toothpicks in a two-dimensional structure of almost any shape by gluing them together with quick-drying glue. Leave them in place until dry. They may have to be torn off the newspaper, and the paper picked off the glue. Toothpicks may be broken and used in shorter pieces. Older children can build very complex three-dimensional structures this way, but preschoolers seldom have the patience required for the drying time.

For added decoration, glue a piece of cellophane or tissue paper here and there over some of the frames of toothpicks within the structure. Cut the paper a bit larger than the frame. Put glue on the toothpicks forming the frame. Lay on the paper and let dry. Trim off the edges of the paper with scissors.

More mobiles. Make cellophane butterflies by cutting rectangles of cellophane about 4" × 6". Gather across the middle to form two wings, wrap with thread and hang.

Glue two sheets of different-colored construction paper together and cut out spirals as described in chapter 2, Paper Cutting. Hang by running a knotted thread through the center.

Glue or staple two strips of contrasting construction paper to each other at right angles. Fold the bottom one back across the top one, then fold that one back across the first fold, repeating the crossfolding until you reach the end of the strips. Glue or staple them together at the top and trim off any excess. To hang the structure, run a knotted thread through the top two layers of the strips.

Make see-through hangings by using nylon net and construction paper. Cut two pieces of construction paper together in any chosen shape, such as a star. Cut out the center of the two stars, forming two star-shaped frames and cut a piece of nylon net about the size of the stars. Put glue on one star frame, lay the nylon net over it, and place the other frame on top. When dry, trim the excess nylon net off the edges and hang by a knotted thread.

To make three-dimensional birds, fish, and animals fold a piece of construction paper in half and draw the creature so that the fold forms its back. You may glue on wings, fins, heads, ears, and tails cut from the same or contrasting paper. Give wings and fins a feathered or finny appearance by fringing the ends. Find the balancing point of the creature by moving it back and forth on a pencil point until it will hold the proper position. Mark this point and run a knotted thread through it.

String balloons. Blow up a balloon for the child and give it to him together with a bowl of white glue and some pieces of string the length of your arm. Have the child dip a piece of string in the glue and squeeze some of it off by running the string between his fingers. Have him wrap it around the balloon. He does this with all the string, wrapping it in different directions until the balloon is well covered. Hang it by a string to dry. The next day let out the air and remove the balloon.

CHAPTER 4

music,
drama,
and
puppetry

Music is a natural means of communication. Whether an adult is waltzing with a baby in his arms or is singing to a child at bedtime, whether a group of four year olds is marching in a spontaneous parade or a family is singing while on a Sunday drive, the result will be to draw individuals together and to stimulate creative activity.

SINGING

Rhythm games. You can develop a child's seemingly natural love for singing and dancing with a few simple games. Recreate familiar sounds through their rhythm, such as chanting with a child, "*One*-two-three, *one*-two-three," stressing the first beat to indicate the sound of train wheels. To suggest walking, then running, then walking again, say, "One-two, one-two, one-two," slowly, then quickly, then slowly again. Or you may reduce a

(If hands are folded together with the fingers on top on the first line, then on this last line, the people are all on the roof of the church, and the child wiggles his fingers outside, instead of inside, his palms.)

Singing games. The old favorites are the best of these, too. All of these songs can be done by two, as well as by the larger groups at schools and parties.

Ring Around the Rosy
Ring around the rosy,
Pocket full of posy.
Ashes, ashes.
All fall down!
    (Players clasp hands and walk around in a circle, seeing who can stoop first on the word "down.")

Mulberry Bush
Here we go 'round the mulberry bush,
The mulberry bush, the mulberry bush,
Here we go 'round the mulberry bush,
So early in the morning.

First stanza:

This is the way we wash our clothes,
Wash our clothes, wash our clothes,
This is the way we wash our clothes,
So early Monday morning.

Second stanza:

This is the way we iron our clothes . . .
    (Repeat as above.)
So early Tuesday morning.

Third stanza:

This is the way we scrub the floor . . .
So early Wednesday morning.

Fourth stanza:

This is the way we mend our clothes . . .
So early Thursday morning.

Fifth stanza:

This is the way we sweep the floor . . .
So early Friday morning.

Sixth stanza:

This is the way we bake our bread . . .
So early Saturday morning.

Seventh stanza:

This is the way we go to church . . .
So early Sunday morning.

(For the chorus, the players skip around in a circle.
For the seven stanzas, the players do movements
suggested by the action.)

Looby Loo
Here we dance Looby Loo,
Here we dance Looby light,
Here we dance Looby Loo,
All on a Saturday night.

First stanza:

I put my right hand in,
I put my right hand out,
I give my right hand a shake, shake, shake,
And turn myself about.

Second stanza: I put my left hand in . . .
   (Repeat as above.)

Third stanza: I put my two hands in . . .

Fourth stanza: I put my right foot in . . .

Fifth stanza: I put my left foot in . . .

Sixth stanza: I put my head in . . .

Seventh stanza: I put my whole self in . . .

(A circle is formed. During the chorus, players skip
around the circle. During each stanza, each person
stands in place and puts his hand, foot, or head
toward the center of the circle, then toward the
outside, and then shakes it, while turning around in
place. For last stanza, everyone jumps once into the
circle, then once out, and jumps up and down while
turning around.)

Seesaw, Margery Daw
Seesaw, Margery Daw,
Jack shall have a new master.
He shall have but a penny a day,

Because he won't work any faster.

(The child does a seesaw exercise as in chapter 7, Games, while singing.)

Pat-a-Cake
Pat-a-cake, pat-a-cake, baker's man!
Bake us a cake as fast as you can,
Mix it and prick it and mark it with B,
And put it in the oven for Baby and me.

(Clap hands for first line, do actions suggesting stirring, pricking, marking, and putting into oven.)

A Tisket, a Tasket
A tisket, a tasket, a green and yellow basket,
I wrote a letter to my love and on the way I
    dropped it,
I dropped it, I dropped it,
And on the way I dropped it.

(A circle is formed, with one child chosen to dance outside the circle. During one of the phrases, "I dropped it," he drops a hankie behind some child and then runs, trying to reach the place where that child was before he can pick up the hankie and tag him. Adult and child can simply take turns dropping and retrieving the hankie.)

Pease Porridge Hot
Pease porridge hot,
Pease porridge cold,
Pease porridge in the pot,
Nine days old.

(Child and adult face each other and alternately clap their own hands and each other's hands. As children get older they will make this more complicated by clapping with one hand at a time, and crossing hands.)

Skip to My Lou
Choose your partners, skip to my Lou,
Choose your partners, skip to my Lou,
Choose your partners, skip to my Lou,
Skip to my Lou, my darling.

(The children choose partners and join hands, skipping around while an extra player stands in the center and looks for a partner. When the singing stops, the extra player takes a partner from the circle and the one whose partner was taken goes to the center for the song. Adult and child can simply skip to this song.)

Pop Goes the Weasel
All around the cobbler's bench,
The monkey chased the weasel.
The monkey thought 'twas all in fun,
POP! goes the weasel!

A penny for a spool of thread,
A penny for a needle.
That's the way the money goes.
POP! goes the weasel!

I've no time to wait or sigh,
No patience to wait 'til by and by;
Kiss me quick, I'm off, good-bye!
POP! goes the weasel.

(Two players take turns trying to tag each other on "Pop!" Or children may sing while walking in a circle, stoop on the third line of each stanza, and jump up as high as they can on "Pop!")

Ten Little Indians
One little, two little, three little Indians,
Four little, five little, six little Indians,
Seven little, eight little, nine little Indians,
Ten little Indian boys.

Second stanza: Sing again, starting with ten and ending with one.

(The children form a circle and take turns jumping a step forward as a number is called during the first verse. During the second verse, each jumps a step back. At the end, they all yell "Pow, wow!" This may also be sung as a finger game. Child holds up both closed fists, and as the song is sung, raises one finger for each number so hands are open and all fingers extended at the end. For second stanza, he curls fingers back up again, one at a time.)

London Bridge
London Bridge is falling down, falling down, falling down,
London Bridge is falling down, my fair lady.

Second stanza:

Build it up with iron bars, iron bars, iron bars,
Build it up with iron bars, my fair lady.

Third stanza:

Get the key and lock her up, lock her up, lock her up,

Get the key and lock her up, my fair lady.

Fourth stanza:

Iron bars will bend and break, bend and break, bend
  and break,
Iron bars will bend and break, my fair lady.

Fifth stanza:

Build it up with silver and gold, silver and gold,
  silver and gold,
Build it up with silver and gold, my fair lady.

(On the first stanza, two players form an arch by joining their hands, and the other players go under the
arch in turns. With the words, "my fair lady," the arch
is lowered, entrapping one player who is rocked
back and forth during the singing of the second
stanza. At its end, the prisoner goes behind the back
of one of the persons forming the arch and the song
is sung again until all the players have been trapped.
The same procedure may be used for the additional
stanzas.)

Rounds. Some preschoolers can learn to sing rounds,
first by learning the song well, then clapping their hands
over their ears while singing their part. When teaching a
round to a child, let him begin the round. You come in on
the second line.

Row, Row, Row Your Boat
Row, row, row your boat,
Gently down the stream,
Merrily, merrily, merrily, merrily,

Life is but a dream.

Lovely Evening
Oh, how lovely is the evening, is the evening,
When the bells are sweetly ringing, sweetly ring-
ing!
Ding, dong, ding, dong, ding, dong, ding.

Christmas Is Coming
Christmas is coming! The geese are getting fat;
Please put a penny in the old man's hat.
If you haven't got a penny, a ha' penny will do.
If you haven't got a ha' penny, God bless you.

Frere Jacques (In three languages for the expert!)
Are you sleeping, are you sleeping,
Brother John, brother John?
Morning bells are ringing, morning bells are ring-
ing,
Ding, ding, dong; ding, ding, dong.

Frere Jacques, frere Jacques,
Dormez-vous, dormez-vous?
Sonnez les matines, sonnez les matines,
Din, din, don; din, din, don.

Onkel Jakob, Onkel Jakob,
Schlafst du noch, schlafst du noch,
Ringe an der Glocke, ringe an der Glocke,
Bim, bim, bom; bim, bim, bom.

Rhythm instruments. Anything that makes noise quali-
fies as a musical instrument. The following are not
guaranteed to produce music to your ears, but they help
to satisfy a child's rhythmic urge. And when children
just feel like being noisy, rhythm instruments give some

direction to the clamor.

You can equip a group of children and parade them off down the block, or they can march around to a record or the piano. Some store-bought toys, such as a penny whistle, harmonica, or jack in the box; some party relics, such as New Year's Eve noisemakers; and some household items, such as a bunch of keys to jangle, will begin to furnish the children with what they need; but you can quickly produce many more instruments with little more effort than it takes to find the required pieces. Some children will want two instruments, such as jingle bells to shake and a horn to blow, so make plenty.

Percussion instruments:

Two blocks or two sticks to be hit together.

A can or box filled with beans or marbles to be shaken.

A basin or oatmeal box to be hit with a wooden spoon, unsharpened pencils, or a pastry brush.

Aluminum foil pie pans to be hit together like cymbals.

Aluminum foil pie pans filled with beans and stapled together to be hit like tambourines.

Jingle bells threaded on a pipe cleaner with the ends twisted together and worn as a bracelet.

Jingle bells sewn on a mitten.

A triangle made of a wire coat hanger and hit with a fork. Or made of a fork suspended by a string from a stick and hit by another fork.

Chimes made from plastic lids, tongue depressors, or Popsicle sticks hung by a string on a wire clothes hanger and hit with a fork or stick.

An empty coffee can with a plastic lid hit with the hand as a tom-tom.

Wind instruments:

Paper towel rolls with one end covered with wax paper held fast by a rubber band and with several holes punched the length of the tube, to be hummed into.

Combs with wax paper wrapped over the teeth. The child hums on the comb's teeth.

Construction paper rolled into a cone and glued or stapled, leaving a small opening at the narrow end for the mouth, to act as a megaphone.

String instruments:

A cigar box (or other small strong box), strung with three heavy rubber bands to be strummed like a guitar.

A two-foot stick with an aluminum foil pie pan tacked to it near one end. Two nails are driven into each end of the stick. Then two strong rubber bands are strung around the nails. The child plucks the "strings."

DANCING

Often children will begin to dance spontaneously to music. You need not instruct the preschooler in a dance routine or even in specific dance steps. Instead, illustrate the variety of body movements: tiptoeing, dipping and reaching, swaying, fluttering arms, twisting. Some children will want to dance using props such as scarves or jingle bells sewn on mittens. A child will enjoy almost any music he is exposed to: popular, classical, or juvenile. It may come from the piano, guitar, phonograph, or radio. It may serve to suggest a feeling such as happiness, or a situation such as the sun rising or a storm raging. Or it may literally move the children to expression. Like play acting, its chief benefit will not be developing a particular talent in a child but serving as a stimulant to the imagination and an outlet for emotion and energy.

DRAMA

"Drama" means "to act." And any parent or teacher

knows that a child can give an Oscar-winning perform-ance as he protests bedtime or recounts how Johnny has walloped him. But acting, for preschoolers, can be capitalized upon—not to produce a Hollywood hero or heroine, but to develop imagination and to provide an outlet for emotions, such as fear. Furthermore, not to utilize this natural inclination is like keeping a child from his favorite truck or doll. With a few directives, the children will be off to hours of fun.

Games and songs. Some games have dramatic elements in them as an integral part: "The Farmer in the Dell," "Oats, Peas, Beans," "Little Sally Waters," and others. Actually, any song that has accompanying motions is a bodily representation of an idea, such as "Old King Cole," "The Three Little Kittens," or "She'll be Comin' 'Round the Mountain." If you can't recall or never learned any specific motions for these songs, enjoy making them up with the children as you sing them together, doing whatever the song suggests to each of you.

Making faces. Provide the children with a mirror and challenge them to make the ugliest, funniest, scariest and strangest faces they can!

Statues. The children spin around and around until the leader calls, "Stop." They must stop immediately and maintain the position they find themselves in. The leader determines the most awkward, the funniest, the most graceful, and any other categories he chooses.

Shadow play. By shining a light against a wall in a darkened room, you can set the stage for shadow play. The children can try to create objects, animals, and people by holding their hands in certain positions, although preschoolers are quite limited in their ability to do this well. They have far more fun using their whole bodies to suggest monsters, Indians, and elephants, or to imitate actions such as boxing or dancing. For a guessing game, they can take turns acting out an animal or whatever they wish for an audience.

Using silhouettes cut in profile from cardboard, with a handle at the base, they can produce plays such as *Hansel and Gretel.*

They can drape a sheet across a doorway, put a light behind it, then hold up objects to be guessed or simply take turns being identified themselves. In this latter game all go behind the screen except one player who sits in front. As each child presents himself behind the sheet and is identified, he joins the player on the outside to help identify the next shadow.

Shadow play can be done outside, too. The children can be challenged to try to step on another's shadow as a game of tag; or to try to step on or jump off their own shadows.

From pantomimes to play acting. Some shadow play is acting without words; so is pantomime. The youngest children can act out or guess simple situations. Their tendency will be to act out a whole day's activities, so your job is to limit them by example or by timing them until they catch on. Possibilities are washing and setting hair, baking a cake, building a snowman. These actions and others that are familiar to children are best for imitation. Similarly, children can act out reactions to a particular sense: hearing (thunder, a dinner bell); seeing (house on fire, bird flying); smelling (something burning on the stove, a dog following a trail); tasting (hot soup, grapes with seeds); feeling (wet paint, a cuddly kitten). Children can also do one action in a variety of ways, such as walking when tired, walking through mud, and tiptoeing past a sleeping giant.

Pantomiming can also be a game with a leader acting something such as a bunny hopping and others following suit. Or any pantomime can be presented for the

spectator to identify. On the borderline between pantomime and play acting is imitating an animal, person, or
thing with appropriate noises such as a cow mooing and
grazing.

Similarly, children are moving toward drama when
they act out a pantomime and use numbers or nonsense
syllables instead of words. This is not only funny to the
children (and spectators) but saves the children the
trouble of finding the right words for the situation.

The next step in play acting is for the child to act out
simple situations as suggested for pantomiming, but to
include dialogue which the child thinks up spontaneously. Again, familiar situations are best, such as a
mother getting a child off to bed, or children awakening
on Christmas morning.

Nursery rhymes and fairy tales may be told or read by
you and acted out by the child. This may be done at your
suggestion, but once you have tried it, acting out may
develop as a spontaneous response to a favorite story.
You may begin with pantomime as the story is read with
the child or children gradually assuming full responsibility for the lines as well as the actions of the part or
parts they play. *Red Riding Hood, Goldilocks and the
Three Bears,* or *The Three Pigs* can all be done to a
child's satisfaction with an adult's help. For instance,
while you take the part of the wolf, the child (even one as
young as two and a half) can take the part of all three
pigs. Props and costumes are really not necessary although a child may wish to use a lunch basket for Red
Riding Hood, or may appreciate having a hat or costume
as the basis of role to play.

PUPPETRY

From the time a baby plays peek-a-boo, he is developing

his imagination and learning to adapt to situations through make-believe. Although it may be a pretend world he is indulging in, it is crucial to preparing him to face real-life situations later on. Just as with pantomiming and play acting, puppetry can help a child in this area while providing him with happy hours of play.

Through puppets a child can express the emotions which are frowned upon when he expresses them as his own. He can act out ideas that frighten him. He can make those creatures that give him nightmares—witches, monsters, and ogres—materialize and treat them as they deserve to be treated. He can act out favorite stories so that they end the way he likes best—Goldilocks and the little bear having a tea party together!

Puppets are also ideal for developing storytelling ability. The characters suggest a story. The child has only to announce, "This is the forest," to set the scene, and the story unfolds through the action and dialogue of the puppets.

At first, a child will do best running his own show. Then, if a group develops a classic story, which each child knows well, the children can work out their parts together.

The adult has two jobs: audience (and a very undemanding one, at that) and puppet producer. Speedy production is essential. It is very important to get the puppets made while the children are interested in particular characters, such as an animal in a story they have just read. You may even eliminate puppet dresses in the interest of quick production, although the following suggestions for puppets lend themselves to elaboration. Usually, however, a scarf or hankie around the puppeteer's hand will suffice.

You may make occasional suggestions or illustrations that will develop a child's skill. Demonstrate the effect that voice inflection has (deep for Papa Bear or squeaky for Baby Bear), or the various ways of speaking (sweet and slow for a princess or heavily accented for a villain). You may also show how movements help to develop a play or a character: whether a character stands, sits, or lies down; whether he walks, runs, crawls, hops, or jumps; whether he moves quickly or slowly.

To stage the show requires very little effort. It doesn't even matter a great deal to the child if he can be seen working the puppets. In fact, two and three year olds frequently stick their heads up to watch the audience as they play. A sofa pushed away from the wall, a piano bench draped with a sheet, a sheet tacked midway up a door frame or hung over a chinning bar are all adequate theatres. If it is available, a large box such as a refrigerator carton, can become a theatre by cutting out one long side completely and the top third or half of the other side, depending on the size of the box and the height of the puppeteers.

A portable puppet theatre can be made from a shoe box with the lid off. Cut out the bottom leaving only a small frame, prop the box on one side, and use small puppets such as those made from wooden and plastic spoons, or simply those drawn on fingertips.

Puppets.

A. Carve a small hole in a 2$^{1}/_{2}''$ rubber ball so that it fits a cardboard neck (a small square of heavy paper rolled into a tube and glued or taped), or the puppeteer's finger. Tie a dress around the neck or a hankie around the finger. Draw features on with a felt-tipped pen or glue on felt features and yarn hair.

B. In a small cardboard tube cut two holes in the back at the bottom for the puppeteer's fingers. On the front, draw or paint features and glue on cotton hair to make a person. To make an animal, glue on construction paper noses and ears. Wrap the remaining three fingers and the rest of the puppeteer's hand in a scarf or hankie.

C. On the back of the bowl of a disposable plastic spoon, draw a face with crayon or indelible marker. Glue on cotton, yarn, strips of construction or tissue paper, or a wad of construction paper or paper towel for hair. Use construction paper for a hat or a headband and feather. To make a lady, cut an 8″ × 12″ strip of crepe paper or tissue paper, double it lengthwise, gather it with your fingers, and fasten it around the neck of the spoon with a pipe cleaner or a piece of plastic-coated wire. Extend the ends out to the sides or around to the front to form two arms. Spread the skirt. For a man, roll a 6″ × 8″ strip of doubled paper into a small cylinder, insert the spoon handle and fasten it at the neck, forming the arms, as for the lady.

D. Cut out a figure, such as a clown, from cardboard, leaving a strip of cardboard at the base of the figure in the back to form into a cylinder and staple. Make the cylinder small enough to accommodate only two fingers.

92

Pictures from magazines and greeting cards can also be made into puppets in this way if they are first reinforced with a strip of cardboard running the length of the puppet to prevent its bending and tearing at the base.

E. Cut an appropriate shape from cardboard or construction paper, such as an oval for Humpty Dumpty, and draw on the features. Cut two holes at the bottom. The puppeteer inserts his fingers and pretends they are the puppet's legs.

F. Decorate each finger of a glove as a different character, using colored pencils, pens, or fine felt-tipped markers. The fingers of the glove can be cut off or left attached.

G. Mittens and socks also serve as bases for puppets. Features can be cut out of felt and sewn or glued on, or can be embroidered on. Buttons make good eyes. Hair can be made of strands of yarn looped over the tip of the sock or glove. The sock or glove is then worn by the puppeteer. This method is particularly good for a lion, dragon, or clown.

H. Fold flat the bottom of a small paper bag and crease sharply. Mark where the bottom of the bag comes to on the side. The bottom of the bag will be the face, except for the lower lip, which is drawn on the side. Thus when the features are drawn and the puppeteer's hand inserted, the child will be able to move the bottom up and down so the puppet appears to be talking. For comic effect, lift the bottom of the bag up and draw a big red tongue.

I. Tie off two corners of the bottom of a paper bag to form ears. Stuff the corners to make large, fat ears. To make the head, stuff the top half of the bag and tie it at the neck loosely enough to accommodate the puppeteer's two fingers, but tightly enough to keep the stuffing in. (Wadded newspapers or old nylon stockings make good stuffing material.) Tie a dress around the neck if desired.

Crayon or paint on features.

J. Draw a puppet's face with washable felt-tip marker on the back of a child's hand; let the thumb and little finger be the arms and the index and middle fingers the legs. Tie a small scarf around the wrist. Or draw a different puppet on each finger tip. Or make a fist with the thumb tucked under the index finger and draw the face on the side of the index finger, except for the lower lip which is drawn on the thumb. When the thumb is moved up and down at its base, the puppet will appear to talk.

K. Cut a 9″ square of crepe paper or fabric and fill it with cotton, drawing the corners together to form a head. Tie it around a small cardboard tube and glue on features. To dress it, cut a 10″ × 15″ piece of crepe paper or material and gather one long side between your fingers so it fits tightly around the neck, and sew it or wire it to the tube. Make slits in the dress for the arms, which will be the puppeteer's thumb and middle finger.

L. Cut a hole in the bottom of a styrofoam ball and glue in a cylinder of construction paper to form the neck. Decorate the ball by gluing on felt features and yarn hair or by fastening on pieces of construction paper with straight pins. Use different-sized balls for different puppets: a 5″ ball for a giant, a 3″ one for a pig, or a 1″ ball for a mouse. Glue dresses to the neck, if desired, or drape a hankie over the puppeteer's hand and stick the head over the index finger, letting the thumb and third fingers come out at the edges as the puppet's hands.

M. Generously spread a sheet of newspaper with homemade paste and wad it over the top of a soda pop bottle which has been covered with petroleum jelly. Apply several layers of paper this way, shaping the paper to form the head. Smaller wads of paper can be attached to the head with strips of paper to form ears and noses of animals such as pigs and wolves or to form hats and hair. Allow the puppet head to dry two days, taking it off the bottle after the first day so the inside can dry more rapidly. Paint features on with tempera and attach a scarf around the neck with a rubber band. Make a witch's hat or a crown of construction paper, a Martian's hair of aluminum foil, a cape for Little Red Riding Hood of red tissue, red crepe paper, or red fabric. To make a dragon, wrap the paper around the bottle to form a cylinder with the top slightly wider than the neck and concave to form the mouth. When dry, paint the head lime green with two black eyes on the sides and two black nostrils on the edge of the mouth. Then stuff the hollowed-out mouth with red cellophane and glue it in place.

N. Make puppet heads from the cornstarch modeling dough recipe given in chapter 3. Put a lump of dough on your finger and model exaggerated features. Make a long neck, so that a puppet dress can be glued on easily. Dry thoroughly. Paint the features with tempera and shellac, if desired.

CHAPTER 5

fun and easy
toys
to make

No matter how many toys are presented to a child, he will gladly welcome one made especially for him. The important thing to remember is that a child wanting and needing a new diversion will not tolerate time spent on minute details or exact construction. In fact, the ideal toy will involve him in its production, benefiting him immediately. The following are listed more or less in order of age preference, beginning with toys the youngest can enjoy, although older children may like them as well.

Milk carton blocks. This is a good toy for a very small child (six to eighteen months), since three or four blocks are sufficient for building at this age and since these blocks are very lightweight and easy to handle. Using two plastic-coated milk cartons of equal size, completely open one end of each and insert one carton into the other.

Cloth book. Using squares of the same size, sew variously textured materials together at one edge to form a book. Let the younger child feel and identify the difference between each page: rough, smooth, bumpy. An older child will enjoy identifying the differences while blindfolded.

Flannelboards. Cover a large piece of heavy corrugated cardboard with a piece of flannel in a neutral color. Glue the flannel in place, pulling the edges taut around to the back and taping them down. Cut out a variety of shapes from felt scraps: rectangles, bars, rings, circles, squares, and all kinds of triangles. The children can construct designs from the scraps which will adhere to the board, or create a picture. The flannelboard may also be used to illustrate a familiar story such as Little Red Riding Hood. Cut the story characters out of felt using rather abstract shapes. Or cut appropriate pictures from magazines and glue them to a felt backing. You may prefer to draw and color the pictures needed, glue them to felt, and cut them out.

Flannelboard doll. Cut out a simple doll from pale pink felt and add features, cut from felt and glued on, making the figure resemble in color and style the child whose toy it is to be. Glue the doll to a flannel-covered cardboard backing. Cut out clothes for it from felt, flannel, cotton knit, or net gauze. The child may then dress it in layers: underwear, dress or suit, coat, leggings, socks, shoes, boots, and hat. It may be especially fun for the doll to have clothes resembling the child's.

Shoe box fun. Shoe boxes can be used in a variety of ways. One possibility is a train in which several boxes are strung together. Each box may be loaded with a different type of freight, such as beans. One box may serve as a passenger car for dolls.

A covered wagon can be made by taping a rectangle of construction paper over an open box to form the arched cover and attaching four construction paper wheels with straight brass paper fasteners or pins.

A steam boat is formed by inserting paper towel tubes

or construction paper tubes into holes in the top of the shoe box.

To make a jeep, cut the box top in half and fit one half back on the box. Attach a plastic coffee can lid, also halved, to the cut edge of the shoe box lid to form a windshield. Add wheels as for the covered wagon or, for a really durable toy, mount the box on an old roller skate.

A long string tied through a hole in the front of these toys allows them to be pulled about.

Matching. The youngest child can arrange similarly colored items such as fabric scraps, spools of thread, or buttons according to their proper color group. He will not only learn the names of colors in this way but the variety of shades in the spectrum.

A young child will also enjoy matching different items of similar color such as a spool of blue thread with a blue button. Or he can be given a pile of screws, nails, and different kinds of bolts to sort.

A slightly older child can match items by the initial sound of their names: spoon, spatula, stirrer.

A rose-colored world. Tape a piece of colored cellophane to the child's forehead so it hangs over one eye or both. By overlaying the primary colors (red, yellow, blue), he will see how they produce the secondary colors (orange, green, purple).

Lacing. Save an old shoe, preferably a tennis shoe with large eyelets. Tie half a black lace and half a white lace together and thread them into the bottom two eyelets. Demonstrate how the laces are crossed and threaded into the eyelets. Using two colors will make both lacing and tying easier for a child. Be sure the child points the toe away from himself.

Threading. "Necklaces" can be made by the very young by threading doughnut-shaped cereal pieces, pieces of drinking straws, empty spools of thread, or a combination of these on a piece of string or a shoelace. If string is used, paint one end with fingernail polish to make threading easier.

Unraveling and unscrewing. An old mitten or sock to be unraveled can be a toddler's toy. He may even be able to wind the unraveled yarn into a ball. Similarly, a young child will enjoy tackling the intricacy of taking apart a nut and bolt. Show him how it comes apart and be sure it works easily. He will be able to disassemble it long before he can put it together. Or provide the child with a set of different-sized jars with lids so he can match lids to jars.

Telephones. Two paper cups, attached by a string threaded through a hole in the bottom of each and knotted, can serve as the receiver and mouthpiece of a telephone. For older children, connect two tin cans with heavy twine forced through a hole in the bottom of each can and knotted to hold it in place. Pull the line taut. The twine can be as long as fifteen feet and still carry a child's voice.

Button-up bear. Cut out the parts of a bear from pieces of brown felt—arms, legs, body, and head. Attach them to each other with a variety of fasteners, using buttons for the arms, a snap for the head, and hooks for the legs, so the child may take the doll apart and reassemble it as a step toward learning to dress himself.

Mystery bag. Put some toys in a laundry bag or a pillow case and let the child discover what is inside by feeling the bag. Start with one or two easy items and gradually make this guessing game more difficult.

Pet toys. If you have small kittens or puppies in the house and are trying to teach a two to four year old how to handle (or not handle) them, try one of these ideas. Tie a piece of paper tissue or a paper napkin to the end of a one to two foot string so that it can be fluttered in front of a kitten and he will be tempted to paw at it and play with it. Jerk it across the floor in front of him so he can play at hunting it. After you show the child how to move the string, let him do it.

Find a small carton or shoe box to make a pet house. Cut a small door in each end and, perhaps, a window in the side. Put it on a soft surface—a rug or rags or old towel—near the exploring kittens or puppies and watch them approach it, sniff around it, and eventually go in. They may curl up inside or play tag with each other through the doors and windows while you and the children watch.

Yarn dolls.

Woman: Wrap yarn lengthwise around a 3″ × 5″ piece of cardboard twenty times. Loop a short piece of yarn around one end, tie it, and remove the yarn from the cardboard. Tie another short piece of yarn three-fourths inch from the knotted end to form a head.

Wrap more yarn sideways around the cardboard ten times and slip the yarn off. Near each end, tie short pieces of yarn and then snip through the loops. Slip this section through the body, push it up under the head to form the arms, and tie a piece of yarn below it, to hold it in place and form a waist. Snip through the bottom of the large loop to form a skirt.

Man: Follow the directions above. After putting the arms in place, carefully divide the yarn below the waist into two equal parts. Tie each part with short pieces of yarn close to the bottom of the loops, forming legs and feet.

Large yarn doll. Follow the same principle as above, but use heavy rug yarn and wrap it around a 14″ × 9⁶/₂″ shirt cardboard lengthwise forty times to form the head, body, and legs; crosswise twenty times to form the arms. Use a styrofoam ball ($2^1/_2$″, 3″, or $3^1/_2$″) to give the head its shape, and carefully distribute the yarn around it. Tie the yarn tightly in place at the bottom. Insert a fine wire into the yarn for the arms and braid the yarn, tying it at both ends to hold it in place and form hands. Insert the arms under the head, and tie the waist yarn under them to hold them in place. Divide the remaining body yarn into two parts. Insert a wire in each part and braid each to form two legs. Tie off the end of each to form the feet. Glue felt features to the face. Attach yarn hair in a contrasting color by inserting a short piece of yarn (two inches long for a boy, eight inches or more for a girl) into the top of the head, laying the hair yarn across it, and tying it in place. These dolls may be dressed in dresses or skirts, glued or sewn on. They may be made in odd colors (purple or lemon yellow) with huge heads (four inches or more) and several legs formed by dividing and braiding the body yarn (wrapped sixty times) accordingly.

Clothespin people. Because there is little working space on something as small as a clothespin—especially when it's being held by a chubby hand—the child will find it easiest to paint on features with felt tip pens. He can glue

on yarn for hair and use another clothespin as a stand. Children can make a whole army of soldiers in a short time or enjoy dressing dolls in scraps of material glued in place.

Pipecleaner dolls.

Mother doll: Use three pipe cleaners. Make a loop in one for the head and twist the end to secure it. Extend the remaining piece of pipe cleaner down to form a short neck, then bend it to the left. Twist what remains around this arm and let it extend to the right. You should now have two arms of equal length. Hook the second pipe cleaner where the arms meet the neck. About one-fifth of the way down the pipe cleaner, bend it to form a triangular skirt and twist the remaining pipe cleaner back around the torso. Loop the third pipe cleaner around the base of the skirt, extend it down one quarter of the length of the pipe cleaner, and twist it back up to loop over the skirt. Repeat, so that two legs are formed. Using a colored pipe cleaner for the skirt will dress Mother up.

Father doll: Use three pipe cleaners. Form Father's head and arms the same as Mother's. Then take the other two pipe cleaners, fasten them around his neck, and twist them together for an inch and a half to form the body. Spread them for the legs, and form a loop at the end of each for the feet.

Child doll: Use two pipe cleaners. The head, neck, and arms of the child are formed the same way as the mother's, except that the pipe cleaner twists back to the neck after forming the second arm and extends down to the waist. Hook a second pipe cleaner around the neck and twist it around the torso. Where the first pipe cleaner ends, form a leg with a loop for a foot. Twist the remaining pipe cleaner back up the leg and form the second leg in the same way.

Dog doll: Use two pipe cleaners. Form a head; a nose

and ear alone will suggest the profile. Extend the remaining pipe cleaner down and back to form the neck and back, then up in a loop to form the tail. Attach a second pipe cleaner to this loop and form another loop, extending it down for the hind leg. Twist the pipe cleaner along the back almost to the neck. Form a third loop for the front leg and secure it around the neck.

Any shape can be formed from a pipe cleaner. Supply the child with an assortment of white and colored pipe cleaners and let him bend them freely.

A house for paper dolls. You'll need a scrapbook and a lot of women's magazines. Open the scrapbook, stand it upright, and spread the pages. Two facing pages of the scrapbook form a room. Pages one and two can be the living room, three and four the dining room, and so on. Look for pictures of the appropriate furniture for each room; cut them out and glue them on the scrapbook pages. In a large scrapbook you can make a house, a school, a church, and a store or two. When playtime is over, put the scrapbook away, complete with glued-in furniture. The scrapbook doll house will be ready for instant play another day.

Plastic "paper" doll. Draw a pattern of a boy or girl and tape it to a large white plastic bleach or dish detergent bottle. Cut around the pattern, leaving the base of the bottle attached to the doll's feet so it will stand freely. For easier cutting, first fill the bottle with very hot water from the faucet, let it stand a minute, and pour it out. This will make the plastic much more flexible.

Draw features with an indelible felt-tipped or ball point pen or pens (red for mouth, black for eyes and nostrils), or use India ink, and add yarn or felt hair. Dress the doll in any of the following ways: Cut clothes from colored construction paper leaving tabs to hook over the doll's shoulders. Or cut a simple playsuit or sundress from a double fold of a rather stiff piece of material, slitting a hole in the center of the fold for inserting the doll's head. Or iron fabric stiffener with iron-on backing to a piece of cloth. Cut out the dress or suit, leaving long shoulder tabs. Sew snaps to the tabs so they can be looped in back of the doll and fastened together. Sew on rickrack, buttons, and other details, if you wish.

Do-it-in-a-hurry doll house. Boys as well as girls enjoy doll houses. Use a large carton for the house. Trim down the sides so children's short arms can reach easily to the bottom. You can tape pieces of cardboard across it for partitions, but it's not necessary, for children immediately acquire the notion of room areas.

We have tried folded-paper (origami) furniture, but, it is best for older children who will enjoy folding it for themselves. For the two to five year olds, furniture made from typing paper folded several times and stapled into place is more sturdy. We have made the family out of both yarn and pipe cleaners, scaling the dolls to the size of the house. Yarn dolls seem to last longer, but pipe cleaner dolls are more adaptable to sitting and standing, and certainly are easy to replace if they become twisted beyond recognition.

Children like a lot of doors and windows, which one simply cuts into the cardboard carton with a butcher knife. Scraps of material come in handy as rugs, blankets, and place mats. The important thing is to have fun playing, so don't worry too much about the setup at first. Construct the necessary furniture as you think up new games to play, using the same carton, furniture, and dolls for school, church, or library.

Doll house furniture.

Bed: Use half a sheet of typing paper ($8^{1}/_{2}'' \times 5^{1}/_{2}''$), fold it in thirds or quarters, depending on whether it is to be a double or single bed. Fold up about 1¹/₂″ on each end and fold down about 1″. Staple in place the headboard and footboard you have just made. Draw pillows and blankets on the bed with a crayon or felt-tipped pen.

Table: Use half a sheet of typing paper, fold it in thirds, fold under 1¹/₂″ on each end and fold back 1″. Staple the legs in place.

Chairs: Cut half a sheet of typing paper into quarters, crosswise. Fold each quarter in half, crosswise, and then into thirds, lengthwise. Fold down ¹/₂″ at one end, and 1³/₄″ at the other end, then fold up 1¹/₄″ of that end, and staple in place the back of the chair, which you have just folded up.

Couch: Same as above, using a quarter of a sheet of typing paper.

Benches: Fold a double thickness of paper, the width of the desired bench plus ¹/₂″ on either end for legs, three or four times. Trim. Bend in legs.

Bureaus, cabinets, sink, stove, refrigerator: These can all be made from paper folded and stapled into little boxes of the right shape. Construction paper is better for this than typing paper. It is easier, however, to find little jewelry boxes of the proper sizes and cover them with paper if necessary. Use a felt-tipped pen or crayon to make the sink, stove, or drawer markings. You can make a mirror for a bureau by folding tinfoil over a piece of cardboard and stapling it to the back of the bureau, or gluing it to the wall.

Furniture can also be constructed from match boxes (beds), spools (table bases), construction paper and cardboard (table tops and room dividers), dominoes (arranged in various ways to make temporary sofas, benches, floorlamps), egg carton cups (hassocks and modern chairs), whole or cut tongue depressors (table tops and benches).

Play house. Get very large cartons, such as those for

refrigerators, from a hardware or department store or a warehouse. Cut in a door and windows and add as many details as you wish. This same carton can serve as a hospital, a cave for wild animals, or a time machine.

Play store. Open canned goods upside down and save these cans and empty food boxes and cartons to stack the shelves of a pretend grocery story—probably a carton turned on its side. Use strips of paper for currency, or use some real coins to teach the denomination of different coins.

Paper play toys. A variety of toys can be made from paper. To make a cowboy, an astronaut, or any other play person, fold a rectangle of paper lengthwise. Then unfold and draw the figure on the paper, centering it along the fold. Cut the figure out, leaving an inch of paper at the base to act as a stand, or simply refold and stand the figure.

An animal is made by folding a sheet of paper in half (for example, a dog) or diagonally (a giraffe), depending on the animal. Draw the side view of the animal and cut it out, leaving the fold line intact so it will stand.

For sets and backdrops, cut rectangles of paper and fold the right and left ends so they meet in the middle. Turn the paper over so the child can draw in the details that will make it a general store in a frontier town, or a mountain on the moon. Cutting out doors and varying the shapes of the middle section will vary the styles of the buildings. For instance, a castle can be made by notching the top of the paper and cutting out a draw-bridge. A cylinder of paper, also notched on top, can be its tower.

Cars, trucks, and busses are formed as are animals, using paper folded in half, drawing and cutting out the side view of the vehicle, and leaving the fold intact so it will stand.

Chains of paper people. Accordion pleat a sheet of

paper and draw a girl, boy, or any creature on the exposed surface. Draw the picture so that part of each folded edge will be uncut. For example, have the hands and skirt of the girl come right out to the edge, or the hands and cuffs of the boy's trousers. Cut out the picture. When the paper is unfolded, the children will be connected in a chain.

Oatmeal box toys. Many things can be made out of oatmeal boxes: standing, they become silos or castle towers; lying down, they can be canoes or cradles. To make a cradle, cut out one third of the curved side wall of an oatmeal box, leaving an inch at each end intact. Glue the top in place.

Doctor's kit. An old purse or shoe box can serve as a doctor's kit. Equip it with any or all of the following items. Label old bottles "play medicine" and fill with a water and food coloring solution or with cinnamon candies, raisins, or bite-sized pieces of cereal. A small wooden mallet for testing reflexes can be included or you can roll a newspaper tightly, glue the long edge, and then cut off the top three inches. Tie this piece across the top to form a hammer head. An ice cream stick makes a tongue depressor or a thermometer. Strips of sheeting become bandages, pieces of cotton are swabs, a large triangle of sheeting is a sling. The child may actually listen to his patient's heart by putting a cardboard tube stethoscope over the heart and listening through the other end. You may want to include a disposable hypodermic syringe, minus the needle, of course.

Parachutes. Cut four pieces of string the length of your arm, from fingertip to elbow. Tie one string to each of the four corners of a man's handkerchief or a piece of lightweight plastic about handkerchief size. Take two strings on the same side of the hankie and tie them to the other two strings around the neck of a clothespin or the middle of a toy soldier. Mark the middle of the hankie with a piece of thread or a color dot. Show the child that if he holds the hankie at the mark and lets go from a high place such as the top of the stairs, the parachute will open and drift to the floor. Or it may be loosely rolled, starting at the top, and tossed into the air.

Glider. Fold a sheet of paper ($8\frac{1}{2}'' \times 11''$) in half, crease and unfold. Take the upper right-hand corner and fold it to the center line, forming a corner triangle. Take the longest side of this triangle and fold it toward the center so that the entire long side is on the center fold line. Again, take the longest side of the triangle and fold it in toward the center. Repeat these last three steps with the left side. Turn the plane over and fold it in half lengthwise. Crease sharply. Grasp the center fold and spread the wings. Weight the nose of the plane with a paper clip or pin. For indoor flying, tie a string to the paper clip and let the child whirl the plane around.

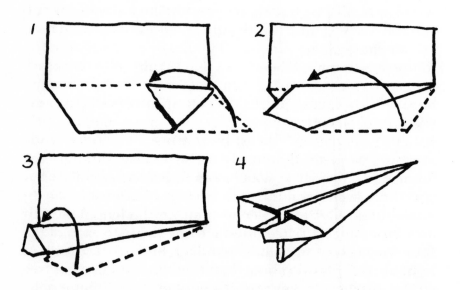

Ghosts. Wad a paper tissue into a ball and drape a second one over it, tying it around the base of the wad with a 20″ to 30″ string, and letting the rest of the tissue flow freely. The child whirls the ghost around and releases it with a swing up in the air, so that the spook floats eerily down.

Clock. Using a dinner plate, trace a circle on a piece of heavy cardboard and cut it out. On one side, draw a crescent moon in the middle, and on the other, a sun. On both sides number along the edge from 1 to 12 in red. Inside these numbers, write from 1 through 60 in blue. Then, cut out two short hands and color them red and two long hands and color them blue. Attach one of each to either side of the circle with a brass fastener. You now have a teaching device for telling time. Begin by setting the clock for certain hours—lunch, nap, and arrival and departure times.

Rubber band board. Using a board about 12″ × 15″, pound in large headed nails in a random design. Pound two nails into one edge of the board to store a collection of colored rubber bands. By looping and stretching the rubber bands over the nails, a child can create an intriguing design.

Bathtub play. A leftover dish detergent bottle makes an extremely good squirt gun, outdoors in the summer, in the bathtub in winter. Eggbeaters to propel boats and whip suds, and containers to pour with and to pour into are very satisfying bathtub toys for two year olds. Sponges may be cut into fish or turtle shapes, slit along the side, filled with leftover soap slivers, and lashed shut with a thread and needle. Besides using the sponges to wash themselves, the bathers may use them to scrub down the sides of the tub and adjoining tile, or may clean up some of their washable toys such as balls and dolls. A bathtub is a good place for blowing soap bubbles in winter. (See bubble blowing under chapter 8, Summer.) Small children enjoy fingerpainting in the bathtub, doing their painting on the sides and bottom of the tub, with regular fingerpaints or with shaving cream tinted with food coloring. One cleans up by filling the tub with water and washing children and tub at the same time.

Make a wild bubble bath with a few squirts of dish detergent (much cheaper than commercial bubble bath products), or add a few drops of food coloring to bath water. It doesn't color the children or the tub, and makes bathing more interesting. A child can see quite clearly the results of mixing yellow and blue, yellow and red, or red and blue.

CHAPTER 6

scientific experiments

Questioning is one of the most important ways a pre-schooler learns about himself and his world. He does not yet take things for granted as older children and adults often do. From the time an infant puts his toe into his mouth until he enrolls in school, he is in a period of tremendous growth—intellectual, emotional, and physical. You can encourage him by trying to give accurate yet simple answers to his questions and by providing experiences that let him find some answers for himself, or broaden his understanding of his question.

Although children really enjoy doing experiments—it is a very adult sort of thing to do—they are not yet ready for the systematic and analytic thought processes involved. They can, however, grasp some basic principles and, when they do the same thing repeatedly, they become aware of the consistency of reactions. Whenever possible, a control should be established so the child can compare two results. Following are some experiments that will appeal to every budding scientist, and countless others are available in science books.

KITCHEN HELP

Many of the kitchen procedures that we take for granted are similar to scientific procedures used in laboratories. For example, an early exposure to the concept of measurement, especially an understanding of the nature of a standard unit such as an ounce or a teaspoonful, will lead to a better and more rapid understanding of the metric system.

Measuring. If you have a set of graduated measuring cups, give the child a pitcher of water and the cups. Let him experiment with pouring from one to another. Then you may show him that a half cup filled twice and poured into the one cup measure fills it exactly. Let him do it. Or give the child two or three glass jars of different sizes and shapes and a pitcher of water. Let him measure water and pour it into jars. Have him notice how the same amount of water in different jars looks like different amounts. Or let him fill different-shaped jars to the same level, then measure the amounts in each. You may prefer to use rice rather than water with very young children, who will enjoy pouring whether or not they understand measuring.

Taste and smell. Set out several small dishes of foods for the child to taste—sugar, salt, flour, baking soda, vinegar, oil. Let him describe the differences to you. He might enjoy the game of identifying by taste and smell while his eyes are closed. Likewise, let him explore the spice cabinet by smell, or by tasting in minute amounts under careful supervision. (Some spices, such as nutmeg, are dangerous when consumed in quantity.)

Learning by helping. The following are some ways a

preschooler can actually help in a kitchen. All you have to give him is a demonstration and sufficient time.

grating coconut, cabbage, etc.

chopping nuts, onions, etc.

stirring with a long, wooden spoon

adding ingredients already measured

making drop cookies and molded cookies; cutting out cookies with cookie cutters

sifting flour

measuring sugar (brown is easier to handle and pack)

peeling carrots

scrubbing potatoes

washing or drying a few dishes

grinding food

setting the table

salting popcorn

shaking food to be fried, such as chicken, in a bag of seasoned flour

Similarly a preschooler can learn to do other household chores, not so much for the sake of developing responsibility as for the experience of doing. For him a mop still has glamour. He can sponge the floor, run the vacuum cleaner (incidentally helping him overcome his fear of it as he learns to control it), make his bed, wash windows, mirrors and glass table tops, and dust. Letting a child help clean up after a spill makes everyone feel better about it. The preschooler can become a cook of sorts, too. He can help make sandwiches, punch, eggnogs, instant pudding, toast, milk shakes, and ice cream sodas.

CHEMISTRY

To children the experiments of chemistry are only a step

away from the tricks of a magician. Exploring the world of science can lead a child to reflecting about his world and to enjoying it more. Success depends on having the equipment set up and being ready to help in observing what occurs.

Fire: A safe introduction to a dangerous subject. Fire, like many dangerous things, should be introduced under circumstances that can be carefully supervised. If a fascinated three or four year old wants to light matches, give him large wooden ones and teach him to do it properly, letting it be strictly understood that he is to do so only when he is with an adult. In addition to the experiments which follow, candlelight at meals and trashburning are two everyday experiences which help to satisfy a child's need for experiencing fire.

In an ashtray, light a match, preferably wooden, and sprinkle it with salt. Notice the color of the flame. Sprinkle it with cream of tartar, and also with boric acid. The different colors tell that different substances are being tested. Does sugar have any effect on the flame? Watch how fast baking soda puts the flame out.

Put a lighted match in a large jar and put the lid on. Watch how the flame will die because of lack of oxygen.

Secure a candle stub in a puddle of melted wax in the bottom of a dish. Put water in the dish, light the candle, and place a glass over the candle. The water will rise in the glass and the flame will die. The water is pushed into the glass by the air outside as the oxygen inside the glass is consumed. Eventually there is not enough oxygen inside the glass to support combustion.

Put an inch of hydrogen peroxide in a test tube or unbreakable glass jar and add a few drops of laundry bleach. Light a broom straw and blow out the flame, leaving the burning coal on the end. Quickly stick the burnt end of the straw in the jar above the liquid and watch it flame again. Bleach and peroxide, when combined, release pure oxygen which makes the straw burn faster than oxygen mixed with the other gasses of room air.

Write on a piece of good quality paper with vinegar or lemon juice and hold the paper over the flame of a candle which may be put in a sink or large basin for safety. The writing will become visible. Have fun writing secret messages this way.

Water. Half fill an unbreakable glass jar with boiling water, add two ice cubes, and screw on the lid. The water will condense rapidly, collect on the inside of the lid, and begin to "rain" down the sides of the jar.

Put a celery stalk or a carrot stick in salted water for several hours and see how the salt draws the water out of the vegetable, making it wilt. Similarly, cut equal-sized potato cubes and put one in a solution of highly salted water and one in plain water. After several hours, one will be smaller. Which one and why?

As soon as it starts to rain, have the child put a pan outside and when the rain stops, measure its depth to determine how much water actually fell. Compare your result with the weather report on television or radio.

Different substances absorb water at different rates of speed. Use a piece of blotting paper and a piece of typing paper of the same size. Put both in water up to the same level at the same time. Which gets wet faster? Why? Will powdered sugar absorb water as fast as granulated sugar? Compare a lump of dry clay and a pile of sand of about the same volume.

Cut several 3″ strips of filter paper or very absorbent paper toweling, hang each by a paper clip in a small drinking glass so the bottom of each strip is just above the inside bottom of each glass. Fill the glasses with different substances until the liquid just touches the bottom of the strip. Watch the different rates of absorption. Try using water, vinegar, food coloring, water colors, inks, and so on. If you are using filter paper, let the glasses stand overnight. The following morning there will be different patterns of absorption visible in the strips of paper. Different colors will rise to varying heights, and some of the secondary colors will separate so that two colors are visible on the paper.

Set out equal amounts of water in a small glass and in a flat saucer. The water in the saucer will evaporate first, showing that water spread out over a large surface will evaporate faster than that in a small area.

Set one saucer in the sun and one in the shade. Fill each with an equal amount of water and see which evaporates first.

Gas. To illustrate the reality of air to a child turn a drinking glass upside down and plunge it into a pan of water. The inside of the glass will stay dry. This is even more wonderful to a child if a handkerchief is stuffed into the bottom of the glass first.

Fill one glass with water and another with cotton. Then, after pointing out to the child that both glasses are full, pour the water into the glass with cotton. This shows that what appears to be solid is really made up of many tiny parts, the fibers, with air spaces between them that will accommodate most of the water.

Pour a tablespoon of vinegar into a glass of water and add a tablespoon of baking soda and several mothballs. Bubbles of carbon dioxide will form on the balls, making them rise to the surface. As the bubbles burst at the surface, the ball will fall. The balls will go up and down for several hours until the reaction is complete. Try this using two or three crushed mothballs and sealing the jar to get a snow storm effect.

Some fires, especially oil fires, cannot be put out with water. Put a teaspoon of baking soda in a bottle and pour in a half cup of vinegar to form carbon dioxide. Place a lit match over the mouth of the bottle when the foaming has stopped and see how quickly it goes out. Children, generally attracted to firemen and fire trucks, will enjoy seeing this tool of firefighters.

Set out two glasses, one filled with hot water, one with cold. Give the child baking powder to add to the water, one teaspoon at a time. The child will enjoy watching the volcanic reaction, and may also observe that it is more rapid in the hot water than in the cold. When no more carbon dioxide is being released, give him one teaspoon of vinegar to add to each glass. A further reaction, releasing more gas, takes place. Let him smell each reaction. Baking soda will behave similarly to baking powder, but less dramatically.

Your child can use this reaction to create a volcano by first piling up a mound of sand or dirt. Scoop out the top of the mountain and fill it with a tablespoon of baking powder or baking soda. Mix a quarter of a cup of vinegar with 1½ cups of water and tint it with food coloring (preferably red). Let the child slowly pour this over the mountain and watch it erupt. He can then pile the tinted sand over the end of the garden hose, turn it on slowly, and watch the pile of sand erupt from below while the food coloring is washed out.

Acids and bases. Dip a piece of blue litmus paper, purchased at the drug store, in vinegar. Note its color. Dip the piece in baking soda and water. Again note the color. You are using the paper as an indicator of the acidic or basic nature of the liquid. Acids and bases are two important kinds of chemical compounds that act in opposite ways. A child may want to test other solutions to find out if they are acid or base by dipping litmus paper in them. He might try a variety of fruit juices, vegetable stock, pickle juice, or a bit of toothpowder or toothpaste mixed with water.

Solutions. Help a child make a powdered drink. Ask if he can separate the ingredients and put them back where he got them. Why not? One makes many solutions in a kitchen: coffee, tea, cocoa, gelatin.

Make a saturated solution by adding sugar or salt to one-half cup cold water, a teaspoon at a time. Stir in each addition. Keep track of the number of teaspoons added. Why does the water cease to absorb all the grains? Heat the water. What happens to the sediment? Start again with one-half cup hot water. Do you need more or less additive to make a saturated solution using hot water?

Mix vinegar and oil. Have you made a solution? Why not? Add a small amount of dish detergent. What happens? Basically, you get the same result as adding soap to laundry water or bath water. An emulsion is formed allowing the water or vinegar to intermix with the grease or oil. In the case of dirty clothes or dirty children, the water can then carry away the dirt, grease, or oil.

Give a child a small glass of water, a spoon, and a pepper shaker. Ask him to mix the pepper with the water. What happens? Heat the mixture in a pan. Does it then form a solution? Pepper is relatively insoluble. Many substances break down in water either very slowly or not at all.

Crystals. Hammer common brick, soft coal, or coke into small pieces about the size of a walnut. Cluster the pieces in the center of a dish about six inches in diameter. Mix the following: 4 tablespoons of non-iodized salt, 4 tablespoons of liquid bluing, 4 table-spoons of water, and 1 tablespoon of household ammonia. Pour the mixture very slowly over the broken pieces in the dish. Put a few drops of color (food coloring, mercurochrome or fabric dye) here and there over the rock pile in the dish. Set the dish aside. In a short time little crystals will begin to form.

ANATOMY

Children develop a deep interest in their bodies at an early age and by four years of age can understand quite a bit about its different parts. They are interested in their senses—seeing, hearing, smelling, tasting, and feeling. Visits to the doctor have alerted them to the heart; a fall has shown them their blood.

Tongue. Have a child close his eyes and hold a slice of pear under his nose. At the same time, give him a slice of apple to taste and he will identify it as a pear, demonstrating the degree to which smell aids taste.

Teeth. Children need to be made aware of the importance of their teeth. The following experiment will at least draw their attention to them. Have a child bite from an apple and then chew, using only the front teeth. He will find the chewing difficult and it can then be pointed out that the front teeth (incisors) are for biting and the back teeth (molars) are for chewing. Each tooth has its special job and must be cared for.

Nose. The sense of smell in humans is not very developed. Furthermore, it tires easily. While a child's eyes are closed hold something strong-smelling under his nose (a slice of onion, cheese, perfume) and have him tell you when you take it away. Even when you are still holding it under his nose, he will say it is gone.

Ears. Ears serve two purposes: to tell us about sound and about our position. To demonstrate that sound is vibration, put a clock on the end of a table and have a child press an ear against the other end of the table. He will hear it ticking through the table. To show that sound vibrations travel slower than light, use the method described under Lightning to determine where lightning is striking. To determine the body's position, the ear has three tubes containing liquid that exert pressure on the brain according to whether the body is leaning forward or backward, or is straight. Have a child sit in a rocker, or swing, or hold him in your arms. Move him back and forth. Even with his eyes closed, he will know what position he is in.

Touch. While the child's eyes are closed, hold out something with a definite texture, such as burlap. Ask him to put his fingertips on it and try to identify it. Then have him rub his fingertips over it. Rubbing makes identification much easier because the nerves have received greater stimulation.

Eyes. Have the child look at his eyes in a mirror and notice the size of the iris (the colored part) and the pupil (the dark circle). Then have him go in a dark room with the mirror. After a few minutes switch on a light. He will see the pupil is quite large because the iris is letting in more light. Shortly the iris will expand, shutting out unnecessary light. If a child wants to know why he has two eyes, cover his left eye and put a pen in one of his hands and the cap in the other. While holding them at arm's length, he must try to put the cap on the pen. Have him try it with the right eye closed and the left open. He will succeed only by having both eyes open.

Muscles. Children are very proud of their biceps and they may want to know more about their muscles. To show a child that muscles are not only in his arms, give him a bit of food and have him stand on his head (he'll probably need your help). Have him eat the food and ask him why it went to his stomach and not to his head. The answer is that the muscles of the throat and esophagus pushed it along the intestinal tract.

Another muscle that can be made vivid to children is the heart. A child can hear your heart clearly by pressing one end of a cardboard tube to your chest and his ear to the other end. He can understand the pumping action of the heart and its strength by cupping his hands together, fingers and thumbs crossing, and slapping the heels sharply together in a pan of shallow water. Ask him to see how long he can do this without tiring and then tell him that the heart does this for a lifetime.

Bones. Put a fresh chicken or turkey wishbone in a cup of vinegar overnight and observe how elastic it becomes. You can explain to children that human bones are very elastic in babies but grow more brittle with age.

BOTANY

Perhaps selling children a balanced diet with vegetables and fruits will be made easier for a day or two when they discover the world of plant life. They will see the dependency of plants on sun, soil, and water, and our own dependency on plants. They will also find these activities enriching preludes to nature hikes and to understanding of life cycles.

Plants: Water, sun, and soil. Buy three geraniums; put a bag over one and place the other two in the sun. Water the one with the bag and only one of those in the sun. In two weeks see what has happened to the three plants. Most common plants need water, sun, and soil to survive.

Terrarium. Using a mason jar, layer in this order 1 cup of gravel, 1/4 cup of crushed charcoal and 1 cup of sand, washed free of salt and dried. Plant moss, vines, and small plants. Cap with a lid, place in the sunlight, and water occasionally.

Colored carnations. Cut the end of a white carnation and slit the stem half way up. Put half the stem in a glass of plain water and half in a glass of water colored with food coloring. Let the flowers stand in bright light for several hours. This experiment will vividly illustrate how plants "drink" water.

Colored vegetables. Put a carrot with both ends cut off in a glass of water with several drops of food coloring for a few hours. Remove it, slice it in half, and notice how the core has been colored by the water. Do the same with a celery stalk.

Germination. Watch a dried lima bean start to germinate. Put a bean in a small glass. Pack it loosely with wet paper towels against the side of the glass where you can see it. Keep the towels damp. In a few days, the bean will split open and the stem and root will start to emerge. If you do two beans at the same time, one right side up and one upside down, you will see that the stem of the one that is upside down will curl around and grow up, and the root will curl around and grow down. After several days, the beans will have to be planted in fine soft dirt in order to keep growing.

Indoor gardens. Cut about an inch off the wide end of a carrot, leaving a few of the stem ends. Place the carrot end cut side down in a saucer of water. New stems and leaves will grow from the old stubs. Do the same using radish, beets, or turnips.

Cut off the top of a pineapple, leaving some flesh attached to the greenery. Let it dry overnight and then set it in a saucer of damp, sandy soil.

Insert four toothpicks in a hyacinth bulb or in a large onion midway down and rest the toothpicks across the top of a jar so the bulb or onion is half submerged in water. Replenish the water occasionally. An avocado seed and a sweet potato may be grown in the same way by submerging the narrow end of each and by keeping them in a dimly lit place until they begin to sprout.

Get a small philodendron plant. Secure two dowels in the soil and lace a ladder up the sticks using ordinary string. Train the plant to grow up the ladder.

Sprinkle some grass seed on top of water in a cup or

dish. It will grow in a few days.

Sprinkle parsley seed on a moist sponge. Keep it wet and cut it as it grows and as needed. Fill it with new seeds when bare spots appear.

Rest a narcissus bulb on pebbles in a shallow bowl. Water and measure daily growth.

Put a small, old potato with growing eyes in a cup of water, a few eyes pointing up. Watch leaves and roots develop from the eyes.

ZOOLOGY

While small children cannot be given the complete responsibility of caring for an animal, a six-month-old child will enjoy feeding lettuce to a parakeet, having a turtle scurry up his leg, or watching fish in an aquarium. Important to the safety of both infant and pet is to keep each from hurting the other. Caged animals and birds—gerbils, guinea pigs, white mice, turtles, parakeets, and canaries—are one solution to this problem. Another, especially where dogs and cats are concerned, is to lay down firm ground rules for the pet and the child. Be sure the child knows he is not to eat the pet's food and that the pet knows he is not to chew on the child's toys.

Even if he has several pets of his own, a child will enjoy visiting a zoo, pet shop, or duck pond. Often zoos have nurseries and it is well worth seeking out such an opportunity to observe baby animals. When a child begins questioning his own origins, babies of any species help adults to answer factually. Watching a mother cat or dog have her babies, clean them up, and nurse them is fascinating to children and adults, answering some of the queries as to how babies get out and leading to others as to how they got in.

Guppies, with their constant breeding, help demonstrate one answer to the very difficult question, "How did I begin?" It is important for children to realize that fathers as well as mothers are essential to birth. No hamster living alone will produce offspring!

Hatching chicks is especially exciting. Use an old television cabinet minus all its interior contents, or a very heavy cardboard box with peek holes cut in three sides. Line with foil or plastic to eliminate drafts. Place a light bulb inside and use a thermometer to keep the temperature at about 95 degrees. Buy eggs from a hatchery (if eighteen days old at the time of purchase, chances of hatching are very good and the waiting time is short) and place them inside. Be ready with chick feed and water for the great day!

Although children should be warned against approaching strange and wild animals, the outdoors can provide some safe contacts with creatures. For some insect ideas, see chapter 8, Summer. For nature walks, see suggestions under chapter 8, Fall and Spring.

METEOROLOGY

Weather affects every child. It determines whether he will wear a sunsuit or a snowsuit, or stay inside all day. Helping him learn more about weather will help him to accept its demands upon him. Talking about the rain, rather than about the ruined picnic, will not only divert his attention but give him a better understanding of his environment.

Temperature changes. Collect some snow in three containers. Put one in the refrigerator. Let one stand at room temperature. Put one on the stove and heat it. Which melts first? Why? Boil the melted snow on the stove until the pan is empty. Where did it go? What did you see? You can do this in summer, too, with ice cubes. The debris in the melted snow is a rather satisfying demonstration of why we tell a child not to eat it.

Hot and cold. A barometer and thermometer will illustrate to a child that discomfort comes from humidity as well as from heat. A thermometer can also determine objectively how warmly a child must dress, preventing a daily wardrobe battle. For example, below 40° means snowsuit, below 55° means jacket, below 65° means heavy sweater.

Sun. Early in the day, note the position of the sun in the sky—behind which house, or shining through which window. Later, watch it start to set, again noting its position in relation to buildings and other landmarks. Try to do this several times so that the children will see the regularity in the sun's rising and setting. Discuss with them what is happening on the other side of the earth, in China or Australia, when they are getting up and going to bed. Make them aware that it is the earth's relationship to the sun that makes it colder in winter and warmer in summer.

You might run a pencil through a hollow rubber ball to illustrate the angle of the axis of the earth. Or you might have a child be the earth and spin while walking around you, the sun, to show the relationship of the two.

Sundial. Using a piece of wood about a foot square, make two diagonal lines, corner to corner, and at the point where they cross, hammer in a very large nail. Place this in a spot which is shadow-free all day. Set the alarm for 6:00 a.m. and mark the shadow on the sundial at that time with a black crayon. Set the clock for 9:00 a.m., 12:00 noon, 3:00 p.m., 6:00 p.m., and 9:00 p.m. (in midsummer) successively, and mark the shadow each time, labeling it with the hour.

Compass. In the daytime, orient a compass to the north and show your child east, west, and south, noting where the sun rises and sets by the compass reading. Observe the North Star at night and, using a flashlight, show how the compass orients to the north.

Stars, moon, and sky. Walking in the early winter dark or sleeping out in the summer provides the perfect chance to stargaze. Point out to a child the Milky Way, bright Venus, the Big Dipper, the Little Dipper, and the North Star. First, help the child get one constellation firmly fixed; the Big Dipper is one of the best for this purpose. Then lead him from that to the Little Dipper and the North Star. When he knows these well, help him learn to recognize others, one at a time.

To carry over this activity, have the child make chalk dots showing the position of the stars in one or more constellations on a piece of dark blue paper or on a blackboard.

A child's awareness of the moon can be increased by noting with him its different shapes and positions and by having him play the role of the moon while you are the earth. Together, child and adult might also make a mobile showing the relation of the sun, earth, and moon. (See chapter 3, Mobiles.)

Clouds. Children can study clouds to discover pictures in them or note the variety of colors, but they can also have fun identifying them by their proper names. The four basic types are cumulus, stratus, cirrus, and nimbus. Cumulus are puffy, white clouds that are flat on the bottom and look like mountains. Stratus are spread out and low-lying. Cirrus form in curls, are wispy, and often warn of storm. Nimbus, or rain clouds, have no definite shape, but are dark in color.

Lightning. To reassure a child afraid of lightning, or, for that matter, to bring such a massive phenomenon somewhat within the range of any child's comprehension, try to determine its whereabouts. Stand at the window or on the porch, where you can see as much sky as possible without getting wet. From the time the child sees the lightning, he counts the seconds until the thunder claps. Divide the total number of seconds by five to determine how many miles away the lightning was. If he counted to ten, the lightning struck two miles away.

Rainbow. To see a rainbow when the sun emerges after a storm, be sure your back is to the sun and look toward the misty horizon.

Wind. To discover the direction the wind is blowing, show the child how to wet his finger, hold it aloft, and turn it slowly. When it feels cool, the wind is blowing on it. If you have your compass handy, you may also label the wind's source fairly accurately.

PHYSICS

Children are introduced to physics with their first lever and pulley toy—perhaps a towing truck. But the field can be explored further with very little equipment and a great deal of excitement.

Magnification. A nice big magnifying glass reveals an interesting world. Observe skin, hair, teeth, cloth, carpet tobacco, rhinestones, dust, grass, snow, insects, butterfly wings. Ask the child what is different about the thing he is looking at when it is magnified.

Electricity. One simple experiment in electricity is to make a light by connecting a flashlight bulb to a battery with a piece of insulated copper wire. Curl the wire tightly around the threads of the bulb and tape it tightly to keep it in place. Tape the other end of the wire to the base of the battery. The circuit should be completed and the bulb should light when it is pressed against the tip of the battery.

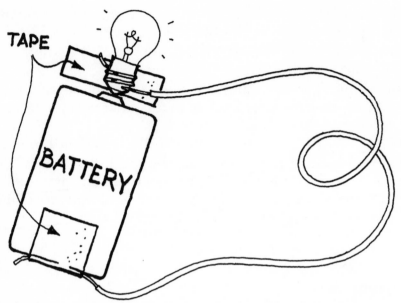

Magnets. A strong magnet is preferable to a weak one, simply because it is much more fun. Have the child test all surfaces of some objects such as paper clips, hairpins, thumbtacks, nails. Which surfaces attract a magnet? Which ones don't? Observe the effect of a magnet on a compass. Using several small magnets (those in the magnetized letters for metal boards are ideal), ask your child to try to fasten them together. Are they the same on both sides? How do they differ? Are they stronger together than they are separately? Place iron filings on a piece of paper and hold it over a magnet to demonstrate a magnetic field.

Pulley. Show your child how to make a simple pulley by tying a string to one of his wheeled toys, (wagon or tricycle outside, truck or block cart inside) and bringing the string around a pole or table leg. Then, as he stands beside the vehicle and pulls the string hand over hand toward himself, the vehicle moves away from him toward the pole. He can use the same principle to lift a bucket to the top bar of his swing set as he pulls down on the string tied to its handle.

Lever. When a child wants to lift something heavy and finds it too difficult, rather than do it for him show him how to put a board or stick under it, place a fulcrum (such as a rock) under the board, and press down at the far end, lifting the formerly immovable object.

COLLECTING

Preschoolers generally don't have the stick-to-it-iveness to be proper collectors, but there are at least two exceptions: rocks and stamps. The former is a natural consequence of a child's play outside; the latter is attractive because of the colors, pictures, and story element of the stamps.

Rocks. A child will bring home pretty rocks or unusual ones from a walk around the block. If he keeps them together in a container such as a coffee can, the accumulation will become a collection after a while. The child can sort these out by color or general similarity of material. By playing with and handling the rocks he can learn the basic distinctions between igneous and sedimentary rock, granite, quartz, slate, iron, and copper. Children enjoy washing rocks, sorting them into egg cartons, and perhaps labeling them—though they may not be enthusiastic about labeling, and shouldn't be forced to. Help a child look for fossil imprints and, while traveling, keep an eye open for specimens abundant in some areas, and scarce in others such as coal, mica, shale.

Have a child interested in rocks fill a jar with dirt and water and shake it, then put it aside. During the day, as the child observes the jar, ask him to describe what is happening. As time passes and the dirt and water separate, explain that this is the way sedimentary rock and clay are formed from dirt in river beds. And this is why fossils are found in sedimentary rock.

A child will almost naturally become aware of the differences between clay, humus, and sand. Working in the sandbox, he will observe that sand behaves somewhat differently from the dirt in his mudhole and yet they are similar. If he is also familiar with clay, he will observe that it differs from the other two. Have the child make a pile of dirt and one of sand of about the same size. Let them dry. Then let him pour a bucket of water slowly over each. What happens?

Stamps. Use any small notebook to hold the child's collection and, to get a good supply and some variety, start at Christmas time. Separate the stamps from the envelopes by laying the stamped envelope face down on a plate and covering the envelope with a wet sponge. In a few hours, the envelope will be saturated and the stamp will peel off easily.

A beginning collector may want to save all the stamps he can get hold of, even duplicates and advertising stickers and coupons. Later he may only want the best specimens. Let him arrange the stamps as he pleases, pasting them in his notebook with flour and water paste or library paste so they can easily be removed with a damp sponge when he is older and more discriminating. (It is very difficult for a three year old to use proper stamp hinges, for he almost always licks off all the glue.)

As the child becomes aware of the increasing quantity of his most common stamps, he may want to keep duplicates in an envelope, rather than putting them all in his notebook. He may find friends to trade with. Or he may want to use these duplicates for some of the cutting and pasting ideas mentioned in chapter 2, Painting and Paper Cutting.

If corresponding friends and relatives know that there is a junior philatelist in the family, they will enjoy helping him by looking for commemorative issues when they purchase stamps.

chapter 7

games

Often, although quite willing to play with a child, an adult is not up to crawling around the floor with feather in hair and hatchet in hand. Games can be the answer, just as they are often the best recourse when waiting in a doctor's office, driving on a vacation, entertaining a youngster's friends at a party, or whiling away a rainy day.

But like some medicines, games can have undesirable side effects, for children hate to lose. To prevent a flood of tears, you can suggest playing the best two out of three games, a less competitive game, or one in which you know the child will win. As a last resort, play a game where no one wins!

All the games in this section require no special boards or pieces, with the exception of a regulation deck of cards. However, games like dominoes and checkers are well within the grasp of four year olds and are worth investigating. Some of the following games are marked as especially appropriate to a certain occasion or age group: P–parties, T–traveling (more in chapter 10), W–waiting. Numbers after card games indicate suitable age.

CARDS

If the child has a hard time holding his cards, rest a shoebox on its side, with the lid off, so he can line his hand up without its being seen.

Feed the Bunny. (2¹/₂ up) Deal out the cards of a regulation deck and arrange them in piles face down in front of each player. Each takes turns flipping over the top card. The red cards go in a dish in the middle of the table; the black cards are placed beside each player's pile. Since the red cards are carrots for the bunny and the black cards are the player's own winnings, even a very young child will be satisfied with what turns up. In fact, if only two people play, there are no losers, since one person will feed the bunny the most carrots and the other will accumulate the most black cards.

Suits. (2¹/₂ up) Deal out a deck of cards and have the child stack his in front face up. He then sorts them out to see which suit he has most of. There are no losers in this game either.

Pairs. (3 up) From a regular deck of cards, select five cards per player, being sure there is only one pair in all. Deal the cards out and take turns going clockwise, each player picking from the hand to his right. The first to get the pair wins. The game's advantages are that small hands have few cards to hold, the game goes fast, and winning is left to chance so a variety of ages can play.

Concentration. (3 up) Some small children are very good at this, even using a 52-card deck. But, to start, choose an arbitrary number of pairs from the deck, perhaps six, shuffle and lay them out face down on a flat surface, so they form a square or a rectangle of rows of cards. The first player turns up two cards at random. If the numbers or pictures match, he pairs them and piles them face down in front of himself. If they don't match, he turns them face down again, in place, carefully noting their position. The second player then turns up two cards, also attempting to make a pair. The players continue to turn up cards in turn, always turning back non-pairs, until all cards are removed from the board. The winner has the most pairs at the end.

Frequently, the winner of a pair is allowed to take another turn. However, this means that toward the end of the game, one lucky player will be in a position to clear the board and undoubtedly win. Since these young children are just learning to take competition in small doses, including good winning and good losing, it is best not to reward the winner of a pair in this way, but to keep on with the regular rotation of turns.

To make the game even easier, have the child match the colors only, red with red and black with black.

Old Maid. (3 up) Remove all the face cards, except the queen of spades (the Old Maid), from a regulation deck. Deal out all the cards. Each player sorts his hand into pairs, matching numbers, such as two tens. These pairs are laid face down in front of him. Then the dealer offers his hand face down, spread like a fan, to the neighbor on the left. This player draws one and if it matches a card in his hand, he discards this new pair. He, in turn, presents his cards to the player at his left. This process continues until one player is left with only one card—the Old Maid. For smaller children who have difficulty holding cards, shorten the deck by removing several pairs of numbered cards.

Fish. (3 up) Deal out five cards to each player. Place the remainder face down in the center of the table. The dealer asks any other player for cards of a certain number. For example, "Do you have any fives?" He must have one card of that number to ask for it. If the player asked has one or more of that number, he must hand it or them over. If he hasn't got any, he says, "Fish," and the first player takes the top card from the pile in the center. However, if the first player is successful in his first request, he gets to ask for cards of a different number, or another player for cards of any number. His turn is over only when he is told to fish. It is then the turn of the player on his left.

The object is to collect four cards of a kind, such as four fives, and make a "book," which is then removed from the player's hand and placed face down in front of the player.

By using a partial deck, such as five sets of four of a kind, or by making books of pairs instead of four cards from a deck of ten or twelve pairs, much younger children may play. It is best to vary the size of the deck according to the number and age of the children playing.

Snap. (3½ up) The cards are equally distributed and piled face down in front of each player. The players turn their cards over simultaneously, always holding the top card, to be turned over, by an outer corner and flipping it away from themselves as they place it in front of their pile to form a new pile of face-up cards. If two cards match, the first player to say, "SNAP!" wins the pile of turned up cards from the other. These cards are placed face down under the winner's pile of cards. The first player to get all the cards wins the game.

War. (4 up) Deal out the cards of a regulation deck and have each player place his share in a pile face down in front of him. All players turn over the top card simultaneously. The highest card gets all the other cards that were turned over. The acquired cards are placed face down at the bottom of the winner's pile. In case of a tie, all the players turn over another card to determine the winner of both rounds.

I doubt it. (4 up) Deal out an equal number of cards to three or more players, any leftover cards being put face down in the center of the table. The object of the game is to get rid of as many cards as possible, so the first player out of cards wins. Each player puts from one to four cards face down on the center pile and, as he does so, he gives a number and sequential description. The first player starts with aces, the second player puts on twos, and so on up to kings, when the sequence begins again with aces. For example, the first player puts down three cards, which may or may not be aces, and says, "Three aces." The second player puts down four cards, which may or may not be twos, and says, "Four twos." The play should move fast from one player to the next, but if anyone questions the statement of any player as to the number or nature of the cards put down, he must quickly say, "I doubt it," before any more cards have been put on top. When challenged, a player must turn up his cards. If they are what he has said they are, for example, four twos, the doubter has to take all the cards in the center pile. But if one or more of the cards is not a two, then the player who put them down must take the whole center pile. Each player must put at least one card down for each turn, whether or not he has the correct card. This requires good acting.

Since this game is a permissible way of telling whoppers, it really appeals to those four and five year olds who are having trouble learning what is allowed and what is not in the world of hard, factual truth.

ACTIVE BUT INDOORS

It's raining, it's pouring. Pouring rice, water, or beans from pitcher to pitcher is good training in coordination for a toddler as well as a lot of fun. The rule is that he holds the pitcher in one hand and pours with a steady stream into the second pitcher. Then he pours the contents back into the first pitcher with his other hand.

A balancing act. (P) On the floor place a long, narrow board (2″ × 4″ × 8′), a strip of masking tape, or a chalk line, and let the child try "walking the line"—forwards, backwards, hopping, and with eyes closed. An older child can have the board raised two inches off the ground by three wooden blocks of equal size nailed in at equal distances.

Ship shapes. (P) Cut large circles, squares, and triangles from newspaper. Place them close together, but not overlapping, on the floor in random order. The children try to step only on the squares or circles or triangles, as directed.

For a variation on this, the leader calls out a list of four, such as, "two circles, one triangle, one square." The player whose turn it is tries to put his hands and feet on the specified shapes, all at the same time.

Timing nap time. Set a timer for ten minutes and hide it somewhere in the child's bedroom. He must find it before it rings. When he finds the timer, reset it again for the length of naptime, telling the child he must stay in bed until it rings again.

Hide and seek. (P) This is an important game for very young children who are in the process of learning to separate from their mothers. Peek-a-boo, with a small blanket, napkin, or hands over the eyes, is the first step. By the age of one, a child will enjoy running and hiding (usually in the same place) while the adult looks for him and finds him. Then the adult can take turns at hiding; at first in a very obvious place, later in more difficult locations. The object is, of course, for the child to have the pleasure of finding the adult each time with a minimum of worry and a maximum of fun.

A variation on this for one and two year olds is to hide an object in a fairly obvious place, such as under a couch cushion or behind a chair, for the child to find. At first the child will believe that the object has disappeared, but as he grows older he will realize that it continues to exist although out of his sight, and gradually will become determined enough to find a book or toy that you have hidden quite well.

Sardines. (P) While everyone else closes his eyes, one person hides. Then each person looks individually for the hider. When one finds him, he hides with him. If the hiding place gets too small to hold all the hiders, they may move *en masse* to a new spot. The last to find the hiding place hides first in the next game. Although a lot of fun for older children, the game is adaptable to indoor play with only an adult and two children.

Stepping stones. (P) Arrange a path of stepping stones, cut from newspaper, at various intervals. The child walks from stone to stone, with only one foot allowed on a stone. A four or five year old may try this with a book on his head.

Hand loop. The child clasps his hands in a loop in front of himself and puts one leg through the loop, then the other!

Fingertip touch. (W) Have the child try to touch the fingertips of one of his hands to the wrist of the same hand. Or have him try to kiss his elbow.

Toe talent. The child picks up a marble with his toes and carries it in hobbling fashion for a designated distance without dropping it.

Racing. The children can race indoors by walking or running backwards, skipping or hopping on one foot, or jumping with both feet together.

Indian wrestling. Two children kneel, sit, or stand facing each other, and clasp each other's right hands in front with their elbows bent. Each tries to push the other's hand back or down. For real fun, the children should be of equal strength.

For variation, have the children lie on their backs with their legs up in the air. Each presses both his feet against the other's. At a signal, each tries to push the other's feet back until the knees touch the body.

Gears. (P) Children stand with arms straight out from their shoulders to the sides. They then turn carefully in place so that their arms rotate in between each others' like interlocking gears. When the leader calls, "Gears out of control!" they move farther apart and spin wildly, as fast as they can, until they fall down.

I spy Googli-eye. (P) A circle is formed around one player who says "I spy." The others question, "Who do you spy?" He answers, "Googli-eye." The question follows "Who is he?" The leader then names one person who joins him in the center of the circle. Both fold their arms and, hopping on one leg, try to "butt" the other off balance with their arms. If the leader succeeds, he joins the others to form the circle and the loser becomes the new leader.

Jumping jacks. The child stands with his feet together and hands at his sides. Then he rapidly spreads his feet apart sideways while clapping his hands overhead. Repeat.

Seesaw. From a standing position with hands at his sides, the child bends his legs, bringing himself to a squatting position, with his arms extended in front. He then raises himself to a standing position, bringing his arms back to his sides.

Somersaults. The child squats down, places his hands on the floor in front of him, tucks his head down between his arms, and pushes himself up and over with his feet.

Bicycle pumping. Lying on his back, the child puts his feet in the air, supporting the middle of his back with his hands and arms. He then pretends to pedal in the air with his feet.

Tailor sits. The child sits with his knees bent out to the side and either crosses his ankles or brings the soles of his feet together. Then he tries to press his knees down to the ground. He may cross his arms while doing this.

Situps. From a lying down position, the child clasps his hands behind his head and tries to sit up.

Pushups. Young children lie on their stomachs with hands flat down in front near their shoulders. They push up with their hands to raise their chests off the floor and then lower themselves to the floor again.

Mule kick. The child kneels with his hands on the floor. As his chin goes down to touch the ground, one leg straightens up and out, kicking toward the ceiling; elbows bend out. He returns to the original position and repeats the exercise using the other leg.

Duck walk. While in a squatting position, hands on hips, the child waddles across the room.

Crab walk. The child lies on his back and raises his body off the floor with his arms and legs. He then crawls across the floor.

Head and hand stand. The child places the top of his head on the floor between his hands which are pressed firmly on the floor. He then pushes with his feet, bringing his legs up until he is in a vertical position. Try this first against a couch or wall, while learning to balance on head and hands.

Wheelbarrow. One child lies on the floor on his stomach, his hands under his chest. The other stands at his feet, and lifts up his legs by the ankles. The first child then straightens his arms and walks on his hands.

BRAIN GAMES

Preposition play. Use a carton and a favorite toy such as a doll and challenge a child to put the toy in, under, on, over, using as many prepositions as can apply. It's even more fun if you have a carton large enough so your child can do this with himself, rather than the toy.

Tumble down. (P) Using building blocks, the players take turns constructing a tower. The loser is the one whose block topples the tower.

Mailing away. Very small children enjoy receiving mail, and a good rainy day game is hunting up offers in magazines, on cereal boxes, or in books that interest the child. Send away for them. If he licks the stamp and envelope, and puts the letter in the mail box, he will enjoy the project even more.

Touch and guess. (P) Put a paper clip, cork, rubber band, grape, or any other small object in a paper bag. The child or children attempt to guess what the objects are by reaching in and feeling them.

Patches. Cut two-inch squares of different kinds and colors of material so there are fifteen to twenty pairs of each kind. The child lays them out and matches them by texture, color, and pattern.

Nursery rhyme props. (P) Set out props from nursery rhymes—a stuffed lamb, candlestick, pie plate, pail, horn. The children then recite or act out the rhyme suggested by each prop.

Blindfold fun. (P) Blindfold the child and give him familiar objects to identify by feel. This may be done with a small child, if he doesn't object to a blindfold, by sitting him on the floor and handing him familiar stuffed animals or other toys.

Educated ears. (P) The child is blindfolded. When he hears a voice, he must point in its direction. Or he must name the speaker. For a variation of the game, present him with different sounds he must identify such as a finger snapping or a door closing.

Shapes and forms. (P) Cut out a circle, triangle, and square from cardboard or construction paper. Set out wooden blocks in the shapes of a column, pyramid, and cube. The child matches the three-dimensional forms to the corresponding two-dimensional shapes. Or the child is blindfolded, closes his eyes, or turns his back, and is handed a form he must identify by feel.

Color cards. (PTW) Using an endless combination of colors and shapes, you can aid a child in distinguishing what is alike and what is different. For example, draw five circles of the same size and color four yellow and one green. Or have the child himself color four alike and one different. Or present the child with four blue circles and one blue square and ask which is different. Or cut out five figures different in form (a square, rectangle, circle, triangle, and ellipse) and color only two of them alike.

Toothpick takeaway. Make three rows of toothpicks with five toothpicks in the first fow, four in the second, and three in the last. The players take turns removing toothpicks. During his turn, a player may remove any number of toothpicks from any one row. Whoever removes the last toothpick loses.

Riddles. (W) Four year olds can become adept at guessing riddles and by five may be able to devise their own. For the beginner, riddles relating to the parts of the body are best. For example, "What has four legs and no feet?" (A table.) "What has a head and a foot but no face?" (A bed.) "What has a face and hands but no eyes or feet?" (A clock.)

A similar challenge is to devise riddles for preschoolers out of nursery rhymes. For instance, "Who went up the hill to fetch a pail of water?" (Jack and Jill)

Or you might quiz a child about the meaning of

proverbs such as "Seeing is believing." Challenge the child to disprove them.

Map making. (P) A child who can count can draw a simple map of a given area, such as his bedroom, or his backyard. He can mark off the paces, making a note of them as he measures them. Then he outlines the area on a piece of paper, and draws in familiar landmarks such as the sand box, driveway and swing set, flower beds, and trees. He may then challenge his friends to find a treasure which he has hidden. He marks the treasure location on the map and his friends use his map as the guide. The treasure may be a small bag of discarded or play jewelry, or candy or cookies wrapped in plastic.

The moon is round. (PTW) With his finger, the child draws a picture of the man in the moon in the air, while saying, "The moon is round. It has two eyes, a nose, and a mouth." The other players must imitate him exactly, the trick being that they will concentrate on drawing the picture accurately while the leader will be inconspicuously doing something unusual or extra, such as using his left hand, or clearing his throat before starting.

Memory. (PTW) A tray of about five items is set before a child or group of children. He names them aloud while studying them for two or three minutes. Then he turns his back. One item is removed and hidden from view, and the player must re-examine the tray and guess what is missing. Or he must name which item was moved to a different position. Or he must name what new item has been added. Or, with his back turned, he must itemize what is on the tray.

Dictionary. (TW) One player challenges another to say all the words he can think of in one minute that start with a given letter of the alphabet. The challenger watches the second hand of a clock, and both players try to keep count. The first player then chooses a letter for the challenger to work from and times him. Young children can do this rather well with consonants, but vowels, with their changing sounds, are too difficult.

Synonyms. (TW) Adult and child try to think of as many words as they can with similar meanings, such as big (large, tall, high, vast, great, mighty) or small (little, tiny, bitty). The adult may want to go so far as to check a dictionary or thesaurus as a way to developing the child's vocabulary, or he may want to use the game as a way to help the child understand an unfamiliar word in a story.

Gossip. (PTW) The players sit in a circle and the leader whispers a sentence to the person on his right, who whispers it to the person on his right, continuing around the circle until it is whispered again in the ear of the leader, who then says aloud what he just heard. Then he surprises everyone by also telling everyone the original sentence. For preschoolers, a simple sentence with six to eight words is as much as they can handle. For threes and fours, an example would be, "The circus is coming to town." For fours and fives, it may be a little more difficult, such as, "Many heavy hippos live in Hawaii."

Double numbers (or letters). (TW) The numbers 1 through 10 are written at random across a piece of paper. Then the same numbers are written on the paper again, but care is taken to place them so that duplicate numbers are not too close together. The object is to draw lines connecting each pair of duplicate numbers without crossing any of the lines connecting other pairs. The players take turns, beginning with number 1. The player unable to join two numbers without crossing another line is the loser.

The same game may be played using several pairs of letters rather than numbers. For older preschoolers, who are working on their letters, make a set of capital letters and a set of lower case letters to be connected with each other.

Opposites. (TW) The challenger names something for which there is an opposite, such as "bottom." The opponent then names the opposite. A preschooler will do better playing opponent to the adult as challenger, at least until he's mastered a number of opposites.

Yes, No, Black, White. (TW) The parent or leader explains to the child or children that they are not to use yes, no, black, or white to answer any questions. Then the adult tells a story, and in the midst of the story asks such questions as, "Did Red Riding Hood see the wolf in the forest?" Children aged four and up rarely lose this game.

Simon says. (PTW) The leader tells the other players to perform an action. The players must obey him only when his command is prefaced by "Simon says." For example, when the leader says, "Simon says, touch your knee," everyone must touch his knee. If the leader says only, "Touch your knee," then no one must touch his knee. The first player to miss becomes the leader. (For a variation of this game, see chapter 10, Travel.)

Mother, may I? (P) The leader, or "Mother," turns his back to the other players, who line up shoulder to shoulder. The leader tells the first child to take any number of any variety of steps. The child asks, "Mother, may I?" If "Mother" says yes, he does as he was told. "Mother" may choose to say no, and/or to change her instructions. If the child fails to ask permission, however, he loses his turn. Possible steps include baby steps (very tiny), regular steps, giant steps (large), alligator steps (child lies down with his arms stretched in front and sees where his fingertips rest; he then gets up to stand on that spot), scissors steps (the child stands with feet together, jumps forward spreading his legs and completes one step by jumping forward a second time to bring his feet together again), model walk (a sashaying walk involving two steps), varieties of dance steps, skips, and hops.

Follow the leader. (P) The children all line up behind the leader, who then walks where he wills, in as diverse and complicated a manner as he can manage, the others being expected to follow him in every action. He may jump, march, hop, skip, wave his arms, spin as he walks, turn somersaults, and do anything else he thinks of. If several children want to be leader, take turns, limiting each to five minutes.

Find the button. (P) While the opponent is out of the room, the challenger hides several buttons or other small objects. The opponent then returns and tries to find them. For parties, use pennies or peanuts in shells.

Tic-tac-toe. (TW) Draw two horizontal lines across a sheet of paper. Then draw two vertical lines, across them, dividing them into thirds. This will give you nine areas, three across and three down. Provide each of two very young children with five like-colored buttons. They take turns placing them in the squares, each trying to be the first to get three in a row, across, down, or diagonally, while preventing the other from doing the same. Or, for variation, each may try to avoid placing three in a row while trying to force his opponent to do so.

Four year olds can play in the traditional manner, one drawing X's and the other drawing O's in the squares. Or the player may choose a letter or number he wishes to be, thus practicing his writing.

Red light, green light. (P) The leader turns his back to the other players who are lined up about fifty feet away. When he calls, "Green light," the players run towards him until he whirls around and yells, "Red light." They must stop in exactly the position they find themselves and hold that position until the leader turns around and calls "Green light" again. Those who do not must return to the starting line. Whoever reaches the leader first wins.

Animals fly. (P) The leader faces the other players and using the name of an animal or bird says, "_____ flys," such as "Alligators fly." If an animal is named, the players must stand with arms rigidly at their sides; if a bird is named, the children flap their arms. The player who is tripped up becomes the leader.

Line drawings. (TW) One player draws a line and asks the other to make it into a picture. This is a good exercise in imagination.

Dot-dash. (TW) Make seven dots across a piece of paper, then line up six more rows of seven dots under them, so that you have a square of forty-nine dots. The players take turns connecting two adjoining dots at a time, the object being to complete as many squares as possible. When a player gets a chance to make the fourth line completing a square, that square is his and he gets another turn. Each time he completes a square he puts his initial in it. At the end of the game each player counts the number of squares containing his initial. The largest number wins.

GAMES OF CHANCE

Spin and win. Cut out two cardboard circles, one smaller than the other. On the smaller circle, draw an arrow starting at the center, and pointing to the edge. Divide the larger circle into six sections and write the numbers 1 through 6 on the rim. Join the circles with a straight pin or paper fastener.

The players take turns spinning the inside circle and keep score. Or they may each write down the numbers 1 to 6 and as they spin a number, scratch it out. The first player with all his numbers scratched out wins. This game can also be played with a die or a spinner from a board game.

Cootie. (P) This game requires one die (singular of dice!) or a spinner as described above under "Spin and win." For this game, you can make a die out of a sugar cube by marking each of the six sides with B, H, L, E, A, and T. These letters stand for the parts of the body of the cootie. If using a spinner or a numbered die, assign a part of the body to each number: 1, body; 2, head; 3, legs; 4, eyes; 5, antennae; and 6, tail.

Each player needs a pencil and paper. Each takes a turn shaking the die or cube, or spinning the spinner. A player must get a 1 or a B before he can draw anything. As soon as he does get a 1 or a B, he draws a large circle to be the body of the cootie. He then adds legs and tail for each time he comes up with a 3 or L, or a 6 or T. He must get a 2 or H and draw the head before he can use the indicators for drawing the eyes and antennae. The first player to complete his cootie (body, head, two eyes, two antennae, six legs, and one tail) wins the game.

I spy. (PW) The challenger looks about the room and names something by its color: "I spy something blue," referring to a blue chair. The opponent has five chances to guess correctly. As soon as he guesses the object, it is his turn to say, "I spy . . . ."

Black magic. (P) Two cohorts are needed for this trick. While one is out of the room, an object is chosen to be "it." When the cohort returns, his partner names different objects asking, "Is this it?" Immediately before he points to what is really "it," he asks, "Is this it?" while pointing to something black. This signals that the next object named will be the chosen one.

As white as snow. (TW) Give a child the beginning of a phrase for him to complete. For instance, "as white as . . .," "as happy as . . .," as tall as . . . ." Encourage him to avoid cliches and rule out his ending everything with "can be"!

How many steps before the king? (P) Standing at the top of the stairs, the king holds a small object in either his right or left hand. The other players, at the bottom of the stairs, take turns guessing which hand the object is in. The king switches hands behind his back before each player's turn. If the player guesses correctly he advances a step; if not, he stays where he is. The first player to the top becomes the king. (In the variation *School*, the "students" move up the stairs to the "teacher.")

Rock, paper, scissors. (TW) Two players face each other, each with a hand behind his back. At the count of three, they bring the hand forward, in a fist (rock), or with all the fingers spread (paper) or with index and middle fingers out and the rest curled under (scissors). According to the rule that rock breaks scissors, scissors cuts paper, and paper wraps rock, the winner is determined and a new round is played.

Button, button. (PTW) The challenger secretly puts a button in one fist and asks the other players individually, "Button, button, who's got the button?" Before addressing each player, he hides his hands behind his back to switch the button or not from one fist to the other, then extends his hands for choosing. The first player to guess correctly becomes the challenger.

Pin the tail on the donkey. (P) Provide each player with a tail (any strip of paper, identifiable by color or name or number) in which is inserted a pin. Blindfold one player at a time and point him in the direction of a picture of a tailless donkey (which you may draw on any large sheet of paper, such as a piece of a paper drycleaning bag) that is pinned up a few feet away, perhaps on the back of a chair. Whoever pins the tail closest to the right place, wins. Some young children object to blindfolds so trust them to close their eyes.

The game may be adapted to any party theme. The children may pin a star on a Christmas tree, a hat on a witch, a nose on a clown, or a cutlass on a pirate.

Treasure Island. (P) An area on the floor is marked out as an island. This may be done with chalk on a basement floor, patio, or driveway, or by outlining an area with a length of string on a carpet. Establish a starting line. The treasure hunters are blindfolded, in turn, and directed toward the island. The other players call "Hot" or "Cold" as the child approaches or moves away from the island. When the child reaches the island he is given a "Piece of gold," such as a butterscotch candy. To make the game more complicated, spin the child once or twice before he leaves the starting line. Or draw with chalk, or cut out of construction paper in advance, alligators, sharks, and sea monsters, distributing them between the starting line and the island. These may be added to the game one or two at a time, to make each trip more exciting. The other players shout "Danger" as the hunter approaches any of these hazards.

Blind man's bluff. (P) After one child is blindfolded he is turned around for the count of ten while the others hide somewhere in the room. No one moves while the blind man searches them out and guesses their identity. (When little children play, have the blind man crawl along the floor for safety.)

Variations: Children may walk in a circle around the blind man for a count of five. When they stop, he points to one, who enters the circle with him. The blind man tries to catch "It" and identify him.

The children stand in a circle around the blind man. Each child makes an animal sound (moo, meow, bow-wow). The blind man tries to guess their identities by their voices. The first person he correctly identifies becomes the next blind man.

The shell game. This isn't exactly the original shell game, since nothing disappears, but it's all guesswork on the part of the players. Set out two, three, or four paper cups, upside down, in a row. Use fewer cups for younger players. Then give each of the two players a handful of small shells, beans, pieces of macaroni, or buttons. One player turns his back while the other distributes four, six, or eight of his counters (the number being in proportion to the number of cups) under the cups in any combination. When he says "Ready," the second player turns around, chooses a cup, lifts it up, and keeps the counters under it. It is then his turn to hide his counters. At each turn the same number of counters is hidden. Winnings are kept in a separate pile and counted at the end of five or ten rounds to determine the victor.

TOSS AND BALL GAMES

Ring toss. (P) Stick three clothespins in a shoe box lid and have the children take turns ringing them with rubber jar rings from several feet away. Or have the child drive three large nails in a block of wood and use rings cut from plastic lids. To score: a "ringer" counts five points, a "leaner" (resting against a clothespin) counts three, and one just touching the box or block counts one point.

Baseboard ball. (P) Place a target about three feet from a wall. The child rolls a ball against the wall at an angle so it hits the target on its return.

Cat and mouse. (P) The children sit in a circle. One ball (the mouse) is started around the circle, then a second ball (the cat). The balls are passed around fast in an attempt to have the cat to catch the mouse.

Ball toss. (P) Any kind of ball (crumpled tinfoil, Ping-Pong, cotton) may be used, or marbles, beans, or buttons. Containers are variable, too: measuring cups, paper cups, egg cartons, muffin tins, or paper bags turned down once from the top to help them stay open. Each container may be assigned a point value. A target can be drawn on a piece of construction paper or cardboard, using circles or rectangles with increasing point value.

Bean bag toss. (P) Targets: Draw concentric circles on concrete with chalk, assigning different points to each circle. Or, set smaller boxes in larger boxes and hold the boxes in place with a brass paper fastener through the bottoms of all. Or, cut a hole in a large box (a suit box is ideal) and rest it at an angle against a wall.

A simple beanbag is made by cutting two 5″ squares of material for each bag and sewing all the edges together except for a 1½″ slit for filling. Use a large funnel or a paper cone to insert the beans easily, and sew up the opening.

If several children of different ages are playing, mark off a separate throwing line for each age, making the lines close enough to the target so that the successes far outnumber the failures.

Tiddly-winks. (P) Each child is given an equal number of buttons of the thin, flat, hard kind. The players can race their buttons toward a finish line by snapping them on the edge with the edge of another button held in their hands, taking turns snapping. Or, they can see who can snap the largest number of buttons in a saucer in the least number of turns.

Cup catch. (P) Equip each child with a Ping-Pong ball and a paper cup or funnel. The child places the ball in the cup, tosses it in the air, and retrieves it in the cup. Younger children can do this with larger balls, such as rubber hand balls, and larger containers, such as plastic, quart-size, ice cream containers. Balloons may be used instead of balls with large plastic mixing bowls as the catchers.

Ball bounce. A two year old can learn to bounce a large ball by grasping it between his hands, pushing down, and catching it with two hands. The next skill is pushing it down with one hand, still retrieving it with two. He may then let it bounce twice before catching it. He is now on the way to dribbling, a technique achieved by some five year olds. The trick is in the child's pushing the ball rather than in smacking or slamming it toward the floor.

Balloon basketball. (P) Shape the arms of a wire coat hanger into a hoop and hang it over a doorway. Let the children try swatting blown-up balloons through the hoop. Instead of balloons, paper plates or bean bags can be used. If little children are having trouble getting the balloons up high enough, hang the hoop over the back of a chair or from a door knob.

Bat the balloon. (P) The children each toss a blown-up balloon in the air and see who can keep theirs up the longest by swatting it with their hands or with rolled-up newspaper bats.

Marbles. (P) "Sitting ducks" is played by putting all but the shooting marbles along one line and then having the players take turns shooting at them from another line. A player wins whatever marbles he knocks off the line.

Rabbit hunting: First draw a circle or form one by tying together the ends of a 30″ piece of string. Inside the circle scatter marbles of one color for the rabbits and another for the trees and bushes. Each child receives an equal number of marbles and takes turns trying to shoot a rabbit.

Very young children can play marbles by just rolling a marble at a cluster of marbles set in a circle, trying to knock some out, or by rolling their marbles at cardboard rolls standing upright in a line.

Bowling. Line up empty milk cartons and have the children roll a ball to knock them down. For four and five year olds, mark a starting line and keep track of the number of "pins" knocked down in three or five frames.

Pick up sticks. Drop about fifteen straws or toothpicks on a smooth surface. Each player takes turns trying to pick up the sticks, one at a time, without moving any of the others. Once he has a stick, he may use it to aid in picking up others. A turn is over when a stick other than the one being picked up moves. Each stick is worth one point, and the player with the most points wins. If colored toothpicks, or varicolored straws, are used, different points may be assigned by color, for example, five points for red, two for yellow, one for white.

Blow ball. Place a Ping-Pong ball in the center of a table. The two players each stand at opposite ends of the table and try to blow the ball off their opponent's end. If it falls off the side, the ball is returned to the center of the table.

CHAPTER 8

outdoor activities

No matter what the season, the outdoors offers exciting opportunities for physical and mental exercise. Getting outside for at least a brief period every day is invigorating to both child and adult. And contemporary concern about destruction, misuse, and pollution of the environment may make outdoor activities even more meaningful to you and the children.

FALL

With its brisk weather and bright colors, autumn inspires a valiant attempt to do every possible outdoors activity before hibernation begins. The last campfires and barbeques, falling leaves, noisy crickets, fat squirrels and flocking birds, yard chores—these can all be presented as adventures to a young child.

Leaves. It would be almost impossible not to collect leaves in the fall. Every walk leads to a new supply to choose from. And in addition to leaves of all shapes, sizes, and colors, there are acorns, horse chestnuts and pine cones, seed pods, and weeds.

Collecting bags. Lunch-size paper bags, one per child, are an asset on any walk. In addition to keeping your pockets from getting overloaded, the child may become even more observant in his desire to find special treasures for his bag.

When you arrive at home, he may lose all interest, or he may want to sort out his finds. Egg cartons are excellent collecting boxes. Some things may find their way into a collage box.

Or you may take a magazine along on a special leaf collecting expedition, and carefully place the leaves between the magazine pages as you walk.

Pressing leaves. A thick, heavy catalog makes the best leaf press. Simply put the leaves between the pages, preferably leaving a number of pages between each leaf. A magazine may be used instead and weighted down on a flat hard surface with one or more heavy books.

Scrapbook. Tape or glue dried leaves to pieces of paper. Colored construction paper, cut in 6″ × 9″ sheets, is heavy enough to do beautifully. You can punch holes in the sheets and tie them together, or simply insert them in a folder of paper.

It's satisfying to identify the leaves, but scarcely necessary for a two year old, whose greatest pleasure will be in the gluing. Four and five year olds will begin to remember the names of some leaves and enjoy identifying those themselves.

You can also preserve leaves between sheets of wax paper. Place one or more leaves between two sheets of wax paper, cover the paper with a cloth, and iron with a warm iron. Trim the sheets to the same size and tie them together to make a scrap book.

Wall hanging. Carefully arrange a variety of leaves and

flat seeds between two sheets of wax paper and press with a warm iron. Trim the edges. Attach several of these sheets together at the bottoms and tops by punching holes and tying them to each other with yarn or string. Punch two holes at the top edge of the top panel and tie a piece of yarn through them for hanging.

Leaf impressions. Pat or roll a slab of clay or cornstarch and soda modeling dough. Place a leaf on it, veined side down, and roll over it carefully with a rolling pin, or carefully press it in with your hand. Remove the leaf to see the design you have made. If desired, dry and fire the clay, or dry and paint the dough.

Fall nosegay. Leaves with stems may be tied together to form pretty and colorful fall bouquets. Unless the leaves are pressed first, they will curl over and lose their shape in a day or two.

Spatterpainting leaves. This is a favorite way of preserving the shapes of your leaves. For detailed instructions, see chapter 9, Greeting Cards.

Leaf animals. After gluing a pressed leaf to a sheet of paper, draw on legs, head, and tail.

Piled leaves. After raking and before burning leaves, let the children run and jump in them. Be careful, though, not to pile the leaves in or near a street.

Pine cone birds. Wrap a pipe cleaner around the middle of a pine cone; twist and extend it down to make legs. Bend out feet. Twist or glue on pipe cleaners or construction paper for heads, and feathers or fringed paper for tails. Cardinals, parrots, ostriches, and turkeys are good subjects.

Pine cone people. Use the cone for the body, clay or modeling dough for the head and feet, and a pipe cleaner for the arms. Dress in scraps of material.

Pine cone animals. Use the cone for the body, pipe cleaners for front and hind legs, construction paper or clay for the head.

Pine needle porcupine. Shape the body from modeling dough or clay, and stick small bunches of pine needles into the animal's back for bristles. The pine needles may also be glued in the spaces of a pine cone, with head and legs added from clay or pipe cleaners.

Weed arrangements. Plan a hike or walk for collecting weeds to be used in a special fall arrangement. Look for bright bits of color and interesting shapes. The tall and shapely milkweed is the prize weed. There are thousands of tiny parachutes in each pod, and the pods make very good boats.

Putting the garden to bed. Give the children tasks which will help in the job of getting the garden ready to sleep through the winter. They can be of real service in pulling out dead stalks, carting away wagon loads of cutoff stalks and leaves, and helping to pile leaves around rose bushes and other plants needing winter cover. In addition to receiving pleasure from working together to accomplish an important job, the children begin to understand the cycle of the seasons—that the apparent dying season of autumn anticipates renewed life in the spring.

Walking in the rain. In addition to being a good way to get an airing on a rainy day, a walk will provide the chance for floating "boats" in the puddles (sticks, leaves, bottle caps or small boats brought along for the purpose), catching rain in your mouths or in paper cups, and fishing with a stick and string in a puddle.

WINTER

Even winter, the harshest of seasons, offers unique opportunities for fun.

A child who is dressed for the weather will delight in being outside. Cold winds require the insulation of a warm woolen sweater under a warm jacket. Snow and slush require full covering of legs and feet: long pants under snow pants and high boots. Putting plastic bags or a dusting of talcum powder on shoes before trying to pull the boots over them will eliminate the usual struggle. Well-fastened hats, scarves, and mittens will ward off the wind and damp. To be really prepared, have an extra pair of mittens in reserve to replace the wet ones.

A very young child will have more fun outdoors if you join him. Plan to do something in particular while outside: a walk to the bridge or playground, an ice-testing expedition, a search for milkweed pods, or any specific snow or ice activity. Keep moving while you are out and allow brief warmup periods when a child can duck inside for a few minutes. To top off the adventure and warm up faster, have hot chocolate or soup on your return.

When the snow falls and the ground has a good deep cover, there is no problem finding outdoor activity. Get out sleds and saucers. If they are rusty or draggy, rub the runners and bottoms with an old candle stub. One and two year olds can sit between your legs or lie on your back and hold onto your neck or shoulders. If you haven't got a sled, try sitting in a cardboard carton or on a large piece of cardboard. A board, especially if waxed, will go well on a steep hill. Very small children like to slide on their bottoms, or roll over and over. You can tie a cardboard or wooden box to a sled, bundle up a very small child, and take him on a quick walk around the block.

You can flood a flat area for sliding and skating by running water on it to form a thin icy coating. When the first layer is solid, flood it again. Build up a thick enough cake of ice to keep the grass underneath from being chewed up by ice skates and sled runners, or buy plastic sheeting to cover the ground before the first snow and flood it. Sled across an icy area like this by getting a running start while carrying the sled, then flopping. Children too young to skate can slide across in their boots. If you live in good skating territory, equip a youngster with double runner skates at age three, four, or five. Once he has mastered gliding on these the transition to single runners will be relatively easy.

Tag, and all its variations, as well as most other running games, can be played on the ice. Crack the whip, played with a line of people holding hands, the leader swerving and turning sharply, can be played with little ones who love it, if it's played gently.

To play impromptu hockey, designate an area near the edge of the ice as the goal and build a snow wall around three sides of it, or place boards or logs on three sides. Then at the other end of your ice patch, two players stand, one facing the goal, one with his back to it, the puck between their sticks. A small board or flat stone makes a puck; and lathes nailed together, a short piece at an angle to the longer handle, then taped at the end where it is held (to prevent splinters), make a good hockey stick. The players say, "One, two, three," together. On "three" they each try to hit the puck in opposite directions, trying to catch it on their sticks and hit it again into the goal. The person whose thrust drives it in scores the point. If both players have hit it together, it is considered a tie point. With one or two more players, the game becomes a team sport. Players are positioned where they can catch the puck on their sticks and head it toward the goal. If you are fortunate enough to have six players, you will want to simulate real hockey, by having two goals and starting the game in the center of the playing area. However, six is about maximum for small children with hockey sticks.

Make a mountain of snow as big as you can. A really big one is a challenge to climb and a good slide. Pack it hard and hollow it out inside for a snow house. Small children can make a snow fort by building a wall, either straight or curved. Forts can also be built from snow blocks made by molding the snow in a dishpan or other container. Fortifications mean snow ball fights, which can be fun. But if one side is being annihilated, suggest target practice, designating a telephone pole or a fence post as the target. Or bring out some milk cartons to be lined up and knocked down.

Equip small children with garden trowels or sand shovels, older ones with small snow shovels, and put them to work on the steps while you clear the walk.

Build large snow men and snow ladies from snow balls rolled around in the snow. This requires very good packing snow. But middle-sized snowmen can be carved out of piled snow, with only one ball needed for the head. All by themselves, small children can make rows of tiny snowmen and snowladies from snowballs piled up, using stones or buttons for features and scraps of material for scarves, kerchiefs, and aprons. Capitalize on current interests by making a snow Santa, Superman or Red Riding Hood. Children may enjoy sculpturing shapes from small or large balls of good packing snow, or making molded shapes using sand pails or milk cartons.

Make angels by walking carefully to an area of fresh, unmarked snow, lying on your back, and swing your arms up and down in the snow to make wings. Stand up and walk away carefully to keep the picture intact.

"King of the Hill," usually a warm weather game, is more fun in winter with snow to cushion falls. One player, the king, stands atop a hill while the other players charge up and try to pull him down. Whoever succeeds becomes king.

Play "Fox and Geese" in the snow by tramping out a maze in fresh snow with two circles as goals. One child is the fox and the other children are geese. The fox stands in one circle and the geese in the other. At the count of five all must leave their goals. The fox tries to tag the geese but if a goose reaches a circle he may rest for the count of five. If there is only one goose, the fox must return to the other goal during the rest.

Sprinkle salt on snow or ice. Watch what happens. Why does the salted snow melt? Compare it with unsalted snow.

Catch a snowflake on a black surface such as a piece of construction paper and look at it through a magnifying glass.

If you look closely after a fresh snowfall, you can find and identify tracks—the large paw of a big dog; the small paws of a kitten; the long, narrow, two-feet-together tracks of a hopping rabbit; and the claws of birds around a feeder. (Incidentally, place your feeder where it is visible from a window. Buy ground corn at feed stores in addition to millet and sunflower seeds and tie on a hunk of suet, courtesy of the butcher. You can make a feeder in five minutes from a half gallon bleach bottle by cutting out about half of the cylinder, leaving the top, the handle, and the bottom intact. Hang it in a tree by the handle.)

Children enjoy looking for unusual shapes in ice formations after an ice storm, and guessing what objects are under mounds of snow after a big storm.

If you live near a lake, plan at least one ice fishing expedition. Seasoned fishermen construct shacks and tents on the ice but for a short trip you will need a hatchet, a fishing pole, bait, a twelve-inch-wide board to sit on, two blankets, and a tarpaulin. Chop a hole in the ice (it need be only large enough for a fish), position the board for sitting, put one blanket on it and sit down. Wrap the other blanket and tarp around your backs and heads, bundling up with the children. When you get chilly, you can abandon the fish and tramp the frozen streams and marshes.

If for some reason your child can't or won't go out in the snow, bring the snow inside. Fill a large bucket with snow, spread newspapers over the kitchen floor, and provide an assortment of utensils. Small snowmen and other creations can be preserved temporarily by placing them on a dish in the refrigerator.

As soon as the spring thaw begins, buy a kite. Then you'll be ready when the equinoctial winds begin to blow, and spring is in the air.

SPRING

March may enter roaring like a lion, but it brings long-awaited solace for winter-weary adults. There is the exciting search for early signs of spring—crocus and tulip spears, tiny new leaves, fat robins. Suggest to children what to look for, and their observations will be more acute than yours.

Here, duckie. Feeding ducks and geese at a city park requires only popcorn, cereal, or stale bread. The children are thrilled at their instant popularity as the birds crowd around them. Watch the geese closely however, for they may bite your knee, or much worse, nip a toddler's face.

Kicks from kites. Despite the general rule that the larger the kite the easier it is to fly, little children will succeed better with small ones that they can handle more easily, preferably tissue paper rather than plastic.

For novice flyers, you may have to get the kite up yourself. Grasp the string near the knot on the kite that joins the two strings with the lead, and hold it up in the air. As soon as the wind pulls, let the string slip gradually through your fingers. You may have to run to get the kite sailing well, or use short, jerky pulls to maintain its height. Now let the youngster hold the string, looped once around his wrist for security, and learn to play the kite on the changing currents of wind. A four year old may fly his kite himself by laying the kite on the ground, allowing about five feet of string, and then jerking the kite toward himself until a little gust catches it and raises it upward. Or while a child mans the string, another person stands off a few feet, holding the kite up until the wind catches it.

If the kite dips badly, tie on a tail. Since a tail is meant to serve as a brake for the wind, the weight of the tail is unimportant and its length determines its effectiveness. You may use rags, paper cups strung sideways at about five-inch intervals, or tissue paper bows knotted to a string.

Once kite flying has been mastered, attach a lightweight parachute to the kite, using only a small piece of tape. The wind will release the parachute while the kite is flying.

String spools. Pass an eight-inch piece of string through the hole of an empty spool. Tie the ends together forming a loop to slip over a tree branch, the end of a clothes pole, or a fence post. Cut twelve six-inch lengths of string and have the child pass them through the hole, leaving the ends loose. Hang the spool outdoors and watch for birds collecting nesting material.

Pinwheels. Make a pinwheel by folding a square of stiff paper diagonally. Open it. Fold it again across the other two corners and open. Cut on the lines of the folds to about an inch from the center. Carefully bend the corners to the center without creasing, and anchor all four corners in place by running a straight pin through them all at once. Run the pin on into a stick, such as a ruler, or into the rubber eraser of a long pencil, or into a paper stick made by rolling very tightly a single sheet of newspaper, gluing or taping down its edge. The child runs, holding the pinwheel up in the air, and watches it whirl in the wind.

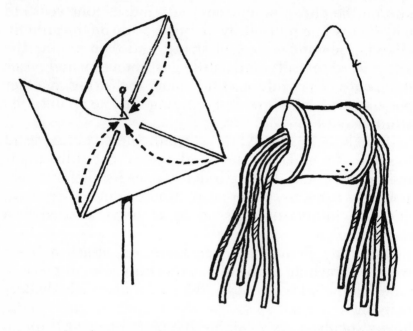

Jumping rope: Snake. Not until five are children well enough coordinated to be adept at jumping rope, but they like to try. A jump rope game they can easily master is *Snake.* Have two children each hold an end of the rope, and while the rope lies on the ground, wiggle it back and forth. The other children try to hop over it without touching it.

They also enjoy jumping over a rope that is held taut and raised a bit higher after each jump. For small children, begin with the rope on the ground. In the game, *Devils, Angels,* one person holds the rope while the others make a circle around him, standing about three feet away. The rope holder twirls the rope around close to the ground while chanting, "Devils, angels." The others try to jump over it; if someone trips on the word "angels," he resumes jumping, but if he trips on the word "devils," he becomes the rope holder.

Skating. Children as young as two and a half can learn to roller skate and by five will find it a good alternative to other wheel activities. If possible, let them start by shuffling around indoors on a rug, either on one or two skates. They will gradually move from walking to skating, and will have a lot of fun, even in the beginning, if you push or pull them along.

Hopscotch. Four and five year olds can enjoy a game of hopscotch, especially if the rules are adjusted for them. Let them use a hand for balance when picking up their stones and let them try to throw their stones to the correct space, but don't penalize them if they miss. They may also have to hop more than once in each square to keep their balance.

Boats. Spring puddles seem to beg for boats. A variety of items will produce a fleet in a short time.

Try half a walnut shell by itself. Or make it a sailboat by putting a small glob of clay (or chewing gum) in the bottom to support a toothpick mast and a paper sail.

Try a cork with a slash in which is inserted a construction paper sail.

Float pieces of styrofoam, shaped or not.

Construct a raft of ice cream sticks or tongue depressors. Use two sticks as supports. Glue five others across them at right angles.

Insert toothpicks in the cork lining of bottle caps. Thread a sail on each toothpick and float.

Cut a milk carton in half, lengthwise, so that the unopened half of the top will form the prow of the boat. To make a sailboat, leave a band of the carton's upper half across the middle of the boat. Make a hole in this band, insert a pencil, and cut a triangle of paper for a sail. Make two slits in the paper sail and slide the pencil mast through them. The plastic coat on the carton assures a long voyage for this seaworthy vessel.

Wagon play. Fasten a wagon to a tricycle for a train, a horse and buggy, or a covered wagon. If several children have brought their wagons over to play, fasten them together to make a train four or five cars long; load one with stuffed animals or cooperative pets, another with sand, others with toys.

By itself, a wagon can serve as any of a variety of trucks: a trash truck in which real refuse such as leaves may be collected; a trailer truck or furniture van in which toys or doll furniture may be loaded, or construction materials such as sand, blocks, and boards may be transported; a fire truck equipped with a rope for a hose; a cattle truck carrying stuffed animals; or a car carrier stacked with toy autos and trucks.

Tricycles. Once a child has learned to ride a tricycle, probably by your pushing or pulling him along for several back-breaking hours, he can follow obstacle courses composed of strategically placed boxes or trash cans. He can follow a chalk-drawn course such as a figure 8, or run a relay race with several of his friends. If he wants to "soup up" his trike, tape one or more old playing cards to the spokes. He can ride it this way or turn the trike upside down and discover that the faster he turns the pedals, the higher-pitched will be the whirring noise.

Sliding. Tiny tots usually slide best on their tummies, going down the sliding board feet first. Then they try feet first on their backs, and finally feel secure enough to go down sitting up. Inevitably, a three year old will try head first on his stomach, something to be prepared for. Experienced sliders will appreciate their slides being livened up. Rub a slow slide with a sheet of wax paper, then tell the children to hold on tight the first time down. Four and five year olds enjoy sliding on paper plates or pieces of cardboard. For bathing suit sliding, run water

166

down the slide from the garden hose. You can put a wading pool at the bottom. You must supervise this as you would any pool activity. All children will appreciate a prior check on whether or not a slide is too hot or too cold or too worn and rusty for fun.

Swings. Children under four will have difficulty making themselves swing while sitting and pumping, but can get some motion themselves by laying the swing against their stomachs, walking forward several feet with it, and then lifting their feet off the ground. Or they may run toward it, throw their stomachs across the seat, and find themselves airborne. Tiny ones can also lie across the swing, twist the chains around, and lift their legs for a whirling ride.

Sitting up, children like to be pushed at the back or pulled by the feet. If one child sits on the lap of another on the swing, facing him, and the swing is close enough to the ground so they can both push off against the ground with their feet, they can help each other to a good ride. This technique is known as "spider" because of all the dangling limbs. ("Airplane" is played by jumping off a moving swing.) Standing on one or two legs to swing is the most difficult way for preschoolers to pump, but a challenge they sometimes enjoy.

Expand the usefulness of your swing set by hanging, besides the standard type swings and glider, a monkey swing (a disk on a single rope), a knotted rope to climb, and a rope ladder. If you don't have room for all of these at once, rotate them. The leftover pieces can be hung on an inside beam or door frame. Canvas swing seats are safer than hard seats.

SUMMER

Warm weather beckons the children outside, giving them greater freedom and independence, and opening up what may seem like a whole new world.

Insects. Children are both fascinated and frightened by insects. One of the best ways to develop the fascination and counteract the fear is to help them observe insect behavior. A way to help a child see a spider as a fellow creature or nature rather than a monster is to observe it as the creator of a beautiful web. Early on a summer day, take very dark-colored pieces of construction paper, about 4″ square, and hunt out a spider web. Put the paper under the web, and lift up carefully. Now a child can study its intricacies in detail.

To watch a spider spin a web, put a captured spider in a large glass jar with some dry grass and twigs and see how quickly it sets to work. Make a lid of heavy paper pierced with many pin holes and tape it to the jar. Don't keep the spider long, for it will starve.

Children can see quite easily that spiders are our allies in the battle against mosquitoes and flies. If they feel sorry for the flies, you might bring up the concept of the balance of nature, mentioning in particular the trillions of flies bred each year. They will probably be too young to comprehend, but you may provide the seeds of future thought.

A glass jar and a caterpillar will produce all the wonder of metamorphosis for a child. Find a caterpillar while it is eating so you will know his diet, and place him in a good-sized jar of clear glass. Top it with a circle of heavy paper cut to fit the jar's opening and punctured with small air holes. Your houseguest will need plenty of his special food, and some stems heavy enough to support his weight.

First, he will make a resting place—a cocoon for a moth, a chrysalis for a butterfly. After what seems a very long time (during which you must resist throwing him away because he looks so dead), the dry, brown, leaflike casing will give way to a beautiful, winged creature.

Release him within the first twenty-four hours after he emerges, before his wings become so brittle that he will damage them trying to fly in the jar, and watch him flutter and dip as he tests his new skill, then catch a breeze and disappear in the distance.

Equip a shoe box with some leaves, a piece of bread, and anything that will create obstacles over or around which ants will crawl. Admit several ants for observation and provide a magnifying glass for the child.

Also, observe the ants scurrying around their outdoor hills, again using a magnifying glass if possible. A child will be fascinated by a tiny brown ant carrying a bread crumb several times its own size. Point out the different sizes and colors of ants, and he will become aware of the varieties of species. You should also point out that it's not a good idea to sit on the anthill.

Make a butterfly net by bending a wire coat hanger into a circle. Tie on a handle, such as a sawed-off broom handle or a dowel purchased at the hardware store. Cut a piece of nylon net or mosquito netting one yard square. Fold it in half and seam the bottom and side edges shut. Fold the open top over the wire frame and sew it in place. (For a quick but temporary job, you can use staples placed between one and two inches apart.)

Prepare a killing jar by filling the bottom of a pint-sized jar with cotton. When ready to use, wet the cotton with a few drops of chloroform (purchased at the drug store) and wrap the cotton in gauze. Drop the specimen in the jar and fasten it with a tight-fitting lid. Always use the jar in a well ventilated area and keep it away from fire.

To display the butterflies, fasten the wings and body with straight pins to corrugated cardboard in the bottom of a large, shallow box, until they stay flat. Then pin them, with one pin, on cotton backing in a shallow box and cover with a dust proof material such as transparent plastic wrap. If you place the cotton on a piece of heavy cardboard, wrap it in clear plastic, and tape the plastic to the back, you can glue on a hanger and hang your collection on the wall.

For killing and preserving spiders, beetles, and other bugs not easily pinned, fill a small jar such as a baby food jar with 70 percent ethyl alcohol and cover with a tight-fitting lid.

Leaf and fern prints. With straight pins, attach a leaf or fern to a piece of dark construction paper. Set it in the sun and, after a few hours, remove the leaf. A perfect outline will remain.

Mushroom prints. Look for mushrooms with gills on the underside of the cap. Carefully break off the stem. Position one or more mushrooms on a sheet of soft, porous paper. Cover each mushroom cap with a glass or custard cup to keep the air moist and still. After about an hour the spores should have fallen onto the paper to make a print. Pressing gently may help, but results depend chiefly on finding mushrooms just the right age for dropping spores—neither too young nor too old.

Clover chains, bracelets, and garlands. The older preschooler can make clover chains. He snips off two clover flowers at the base of their stems and then ties one around the other immediately below its flower, using a simple knot. The one that made the knot is then, in turn, knotted by a third clover below its flower, and the chain begins to form. Several children may try to make a chain long enough to connect each other's houses. The knotting is especially good practice for kindergartners who must be able to tie their shoes.

Gardens. Designate a small area of a garden for a child. Space for one or two short rows of seeds is adequate. Help the child choose seeds that are especially rewarding for size, color, or speed of growth: radishes, marigolds, and sunflowers are possibilities. Follow all the steps on the seed packages, starting the seeds indoors in milk cartons (cut in half lengthwise), if desired. It is especially exciting to start from seeds found in the late fall or early spring cleanup of the garden.

Whether or not a garden needs a scarecrow, a child will enjoy making one. Have him nail a crossbar to a long stick and help him pound the long stick into the ground until it is secure. Supply him with an old coat or shirt to be hung on the crossbar, a scarf for the neck, and a hat to be nailed to the top to suggest a head. The fluttering ends of the scarf and the sleeves of the coat may actually preserve a few seeds from hungry birds.

Shells. Besides collecting clam shells for the fun of collecting, children can put them to use as ashtrays, party favor baskets, or baking dishes for shellfish recipes. Smaller shells can be set on the table to hold a child's gum during a meal for a child, or may serve as dishes at a doll's tea party.

To make funny dolls from shells, glue together two small shells of the same size with half a pipe cleaner inserted between them for legs, and another, if desired, to be bent up to form antennae. Construction paper ears may be glued between the shells, with a wad of cotton or yarn for hair. Features may be painted on with a fine felt-tipped marker, or nail polish, or drawn on with crayons.

Wading pool play. What better way is there for a child to while away summer days than in water play? Although most backyard wading pools are relatively shallow, an adult should always be near to protect against mishaps and to enforce basic safety rules. Keep the latter limited so the preschooler can remember them. Perhaps just these two: No jumping into the pool when another is already in it. No dunking, wrestling, or splashing other children in the pool. For the added safety of tiny tots, set out a dishpan of water or a baby bathtub for their exclusive use. Later this pan may serve as a footbath to keep some of the grass and dirt out of the larger pool.

Whether a child is excited about, or frightened by, the water, games are often the surest way to guarantee safe fun. Fill the pool with tepid water or allow the water to warm in the sun. Protect children from the sun by lotions or shirts if the skin is sensitive or if the season has just begun.

Water games. Have the child pretend he is blowing out a birthday candle. Then tell him to do it again, but with his mouth in the water. This bubbling exercise is the first step toward getting his head wet, necessary for later swimming. See who can blow the biggest bubbles, the most, and for the longest time.

For those reluctant to get wet at all, play "Ring Around the Rosie" or "Pop Goes the Weasel," sitting in the pool on the word "down" or "pop."

Float a ring, such as an embroidery hoop, in the pool. The children toss balls through the hoop while standing around the pool.

Let the children fill squirt bottles or water guns and shoot at toys floating in the pool. They may also use this method to propel a boat across the water. Or they may blow on their boats to get them across.

Make pea pod boats. Buy a pound of fresh peas, give them to the children, and show them how to open the pod carefully along one side. Let them eat the raw peas as they shell them, or pop them into a pan to cook for supper. After the peas are shelled, get out toothpicks, and demonstrate how half a toothpick may be inserted cross-wise in each pod, holding it open and making a tiny canoe. Put two pieces of toothpick in the larger shells. When you have a flotilla, let it sail away in the wading pool, sink, or bathtub.

If splash fighting breaks out, have the children take turns trying to make the biggest splash.

Place the pool under a slide or set a low box near the pool so the children can make spectacular entries.

Older preschoolers can play tag with the pool as "home." Only one player is allowed in the water at a time, and as soon as another gets in, the first must leave.

Put a few squirts of dish detergent in the pool and let the children make mountains of suds, using an eggbeater or splashing with their hands. An eggbeater can also be used to propel a boat across the pool.

Painting with soap can be a grand finale to pool play. Supply the children with paint brushes and two cups of powdered detergent mixed with one cup of water. Let them paint the patio, porch, driveway, fence, and even themselves and each other. Or mix the soap with three-fourths cup water and let them mold soap balls from the mixture.

When everyone is wet, the time is ideal for bubble blowing. Mix one-fourth cup liquid dish detergent, three-fourths cup water and one teaspoon glycerine to give the bubbles durability (buy glycerine at the drug store). A drop of food coloring may be added, too. Use purchased bubble pipes, straws, or empty thread spools to pick up a film of soap, and blow gently. To be effective straws should have four slits cut in one end with the tabs pulled back; spools need only be dipped in the solution so a soap film coats one end. The younger child will do best with three-hole bubble pipe, and will profit from a demonstration and encouragement.

Mud holes. Most children like—and need, according to some psychologists—to play in mud. Set aside a mud play area within reach of a hose and provide trowels and spades. Let the children make mud pies, mud men with stick arms, and build mud mountains, watching the sides erode when drenched with water.

Sand box. Sand has most of the virtues of mud without being quite so messy. Dry sand is good for sifting, pouring, and piling—activities the smallest tot enjoys. With damp sand, a child can build castles, roads, and cakes made by packing the sand in a bucket and turning it out. Wet sand becomes lakes, rivers, oceans, dams, and bridges under a child's imaginative fingering. He can also smooth the sand to draw pictures on it with his finger or a stick.

Good toys for a sand box include discarded kitchen utensils, milk cartons, tin foil pie pans, pieces of screen in a variety of mesh (bend in any sharp edges with a pair of pliers), and trucks and construction toys. Bleach bottles and plastic milk bottles can be cut to make pails. Cut around the handles, leaving them attached to the base, then around the middle of the bottle at whatever depth you or the child prefers. Or cut the entire top off, punch a hole near the top edge on each side, and tie on a handle of twine or plastic-coated wire. Without the lids, the tops which you have cut off make funnels. When the lids are left on and the tops are trimmed down a bit, they make scoops. To cut any plastic bottle more easily, fill it first with hot water, let it sit a minute, then empty it.

Forts. A rather elaborate fort may be constructed by securing in concrete four 4″ × 4″ uprights in the ground. The children, with some help from you, can then nail boards to these uprights at right angles, starting at the bottom. Tar paper and vinyl or linoleum scraps may be nailed on instead of boards. You may make a roof, if desired, by nailing boards or tar paper across the top.

Tepee time. Another piece of backyard equipment guaranteeing hours of play is a tepee or bunkhouse. Drape an old blanket or bedspread across a sturdy hedge and anchor it a few feet away to form a lean-to. Or drape the spread over a clothesline, or a crossbar on a swing set, or the top of a fence, and secure it with bricks or rocks at the four corners to form a tent. Clothespins and large safety pins are useful for anchoring it at the top. A large sheet over a picnic table or over a cardtable serves as well. Or from a furniture or appliance store get a large cardboard carton used for shipping a stove or washer. It will last a fairly long time if you can remember to drag it inside before the rain comes.

The important thing is to provide a safe, exclusive hideaway for a child to play in or escape to.

Camping at home. Camping out with an adult is thrilling for a small child. When the weather is nice, the only necessary equipment is a waterproof ground cloth (an old plastic table cloth or oil cloth will do) and sleeping bags or bed rolls (made from two blankets folded down the middle and safety-pinned together across the bottom and most of the way up the side). A pup tent is useful in showery weather, but detracts from the pleasure of sleeping in the open air. A campfire is an added treat, and a flashlight is reassuring.

On rainy days, the children can camp inside, making a pretend fire of building blocks, going hunting, and snuggling into sleeping bags or folded blankets. A dark area such as a basement is ideal for simulating night time. The children can then scout around with flashlights or tell each other stories. This play may help dispel fears of the dark.

Toasting marshmallows. This is one activity that requires close and constant supervision. Collect enough twigs, sticks, and one or two larger pieces of wood with your young helpers to build a small fire. Find a corner of your yard free from overhanging branches and clear the ground. If a three or four year old is going to light the fire, put a wad of dry newspaper in the center with a projecting "wick" that he can get to easily. Provide him with strong wooden matches.

You may want to build a fire bed of two inches of vermiculite (obtainable from nurseries and hardware stores), surrounded by fire bricks or stones. You can also build a wood fire in a charcoal grill with short legs. You can use charcoal, of course, but it is far less adventurous. You may want to make newspaper logs for your fire. Roll single sheets of newspaper as tightly as you can, one around another until the roll is 1″ in diameter. You will need two or three of them to toast a few marshmallows.

Find enough long toasting forks or long green sticks for each participant. Even one year olds can toast their own marshmallows when held in an adult's arms. Two year olds can add sticks to the fire. An adult must stay right there, of course.

For an extra special treat, have graham crackers and chocolate bars on hand. Place a few squares of chocolate on a graham cracker, add a hot marshmallow, and top it with another cracker. The chocolate will melt slightly.

Sidewalk art. Equip a child with white and colored chalk and let him draw on the patio, driveway, or sidewalk. He may wish to create pictures or he may draw a setting for his toy cars and trains with roads and railroad tracks weaving through towns and forests and around lakes. Put each child in charge of hosing off his art work and, after the hose drains, show him how it can be used as a telephone with you tapping messages on one end while he listens at the other.

CHAPTER 9

holidays

A major holiday looms so large in a child's life that it can be almost overwhelming. This high level of excitement can contribute to the pleasure of a child only in so far as it sharpens experience. To minimize tears and tantrums, allow plenty of time for the child's direct participation in and contribution to the festivities.

When the child first begins to talk about the approaching holiday, sit down with him and discuss what needs to be done, by him and by you, and plan for his preparations in small enough units so that they will remain pleasures and not become chores.

For example, he may decide to make his own cards at Christmas. Plan the design and start well in advance of the mailing date.

If you are going to make an Easter egg tree, start collecting hollow eggs several weeks in advance. The child will enjoy dyeing them a few at a time, he will have a specific task which will be his contribution to the holiday, and he will not feel overwhelmed by the job of dyeing twenty-four eggs at one sitting, most of which you might end up doing yourself.

It is important to realize that most of our holidays are significant for reasons beyond the child's present comprehension. But we can build the climate for their appreciation by developing certain attitudes toward our major holidays. Perhaps you believe Christmas should be a time of joy and of giving, expressed in as many ways as possible to counteract the much too obvious joys of getting. Only by the actual performance of specific acts of giving, and by finding pleasure in doing them, can the child understand this aspect of the celebration.

If one were to observe all the holidays listed here in all the ways suggested, no time would be left for eating and sleeping, much less enjoying the celebrations. The following is meant as a calendar to which you can refer for specific suggestions when you want them. Which holidays you celebrate depends on your geographic location as well as your religion and family traditions.

There are a number of activities which can be adapted to almost any holiday—placemats can be cut in almost any shape, tumbleweed trees can be hung with any variety of ornaments, and windows can be decorated appropriately. The problem is not having too little choice for holiday celebration, but having too much to do or too much repetition from holiday to holiday.

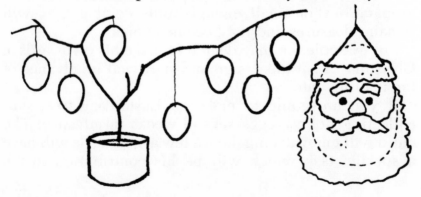

celebrating throughout the year

January 1	New Year's Day	Make horns and hats.
February 12	Lincoln's Birthday	Display flag. Make a small log cabin from playlogs.
February 14	Valentine's Day	Make and exchange cards. Make heart-shaped place mats.
February 22	Washington's Birthday	Display flag. Hang modeling dough cherries on a tumbleweed tree.
February	Purim	Make masks and noisemakers.
March 17	St. Patrick's Day	Wear green. Make a green flower or hat.
March or April	Easter	Dye eggs, fill baskets, make bunnies.
May 1	May Day	Make and deliver May baskets.
May	Mother's Day	Make card or gift for Mother.
May 30	Memorial Day	Display flag. Visit cemetery.
June	Father's Day	Make card or gift for Father.
June	Shavvoth	Prepare plants and flowers.
June 14	Flag Day	Display flag.
July 4	Independence Day	Display flag. Have a parade at home if none is scheduled.

September	Labor Day	Display flag. Watch parade.
September or October	Rosh Hashanah Yom Kippur	Make and exchange cards.
	Succoth	Build a shelter.
	Simhath Torah	Make and carry flags and candles in parades.
October 12	Columbus Day	Display flag. Make three boats.
October 31	Halloween	Make costumes and masks, decorations. Trick or treat.
November	Thanksgiving	Dine with family and friends. Make table decorations.
December	Hanukkah	Make paper menorahs to decorate doors and windows. Hang dreydels from the ceiling. Light candles.
December 25	Christmas	Decorate house and tree. Make cards and gifts.

Note: On flag displaying days if you don't have a house flag or you live in an apartment, children will appreciate a small parade-size flag on display as recognition of the holiday.

NEW YEAR'S DAY

Paper plate hats. Color and decorate a paper plate. Run a ribbon or string through it and tie it under the chin.

This may be a flat hat, sitting on top of the head, or a bonnet, depending on how the string is put in and tied on. You may use aluminum pie plates instead of paper plates and build them up by gluing on cones or cylinders of construction paper.

Newspaper hats. Use a doubled full-size sheet of newspaper, folded to the size of a single page. Fold it in half crosswise. Mark the center line along the folded edge. Fold each upper corner down along the center line, forming a point at the top. Fold up two sheets for the lower brim, turn over, and fold up the other two sheets for the rest of the brim. Staple or glue the corners together.

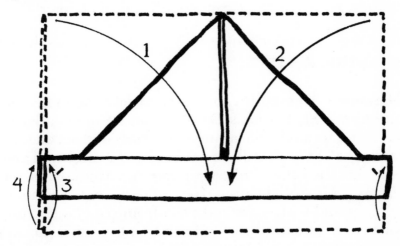

Cone hats. Make a cone pattern to trace and cut around, or simply roll a rectangle of paper into a cone and trim the edge. Glue or tape the long edges of the cone and let the children decorate them with pom-poms at the point, strips of colored paper taped on at random, or however they wish.

Paper bag hats. Roll the open edge of a bag up several times so it fits securely on the child's head. Let the child color it and glue or tape on decorations: yarn, tinsel, crepe paper strips, or, after fitting the bag, cut the bottom of the bag in jagged edges to form a crown and decorate. In fact, once the bag is fitted to the head, it may be cut or tied into almost any shape.

Strip hats. Cut a strip of cardboard 1″ wide that will encircle the child's head. Measure him between temples and cut from soft cardboard or construction paper a shape to represent a hat—a cone for a clown, a rectangle for a top hat—or any irregular shape that will suggest a hat for a Dutch girl, a rajah, a nurse. Tape or glue the shape to the front of the headband and decorate it. Fasten the headband at the back with a paper clip.

Noisemakers. Use cardboard rolls or roll cones from construction paper to make megaphones. For other suggestions, see rhythm instruments listed in chapter 4.

ST. PATRICK'S DAY

Potato men. These little creatures make good table decorations for St. Patrick's Day but can be made all year round and formed from a variety of fruits and vegetables. Stand a potato in a cardboard tube about 2″ high and give your child a blunt knife, colored construction paper, scissors, and straight pins. He can carve out the mouth and eyes and make ears and nose from paper, attaching them with straight pins. He may also wish to add eyeglasses, pipe, and bow tie. Or, if it's a potato lady, a fluted baking cup for a bonnet.

Shamrock placemats. Cut shamrock shapes out of 12″ × 18″ sheets of green construction paper. Or decorate white or yellow sheets of paper toweling with a green shamrock potato print (see chapter 2, Printing).

Hats. Make hats as you would a Pilgrim's hat (see Thanksgiving) but use green construction paper.

EASTER

Dyeing eggs. Use a container such as a coffee mug which is deep enough to cover the egg. Fill it with boiling water, add one or two tablespoons of vinegar and two or three drops of food coloring. If you do the primary colors first (red, yellow, blue) you can then mix half of each with half of each of the others to make the secondary colors (green, orange, violet).

Variations:

Use a light-colored wax crayon or an old birthday candle to write names or make designs on the eggs before dyeing them. The dye will not adhere to the waxed areas.

Put one end of the egg in one color, the other end in another color, overlapping in the center, for a tricolor egg.

Mix tiny amounts of tempera with a few drops of water to make a very thick paint. With a small brush, make drawings and designs on the colored eggs.

Cut small pictures out of newspapers (favorite cartoon characters) and magazines (little bunnies and flowers) and glue them onto the dyed eggs.

Cut eyes, nose, and mouth out of construction paper and glue on, or draw them on with felt-tipped pen. Add construction paper rabbit ears and yarn or cotton hair, and draw on whiskers. If your child has a favorite story (Cinderella, for example) make a cast of characters.

For multicolored eggs, grate or shave crayons onto a piece of wax paper. If the crayons are soft wax, use hot faucet water. If they are hard wax, boil water in a pan. Sprinkle the shavings on the water and let them melt a bit. Then lower the egg slowly into the water so that the crayon adheres to the egg. Raise it again the same way.

To display prize eggs make a collar by cutting a strip

of construction paper about 5″ × 1″ and staple or glue the ends together.

Blown out eggs. Poke a straight pin into one end of a raw egg to make a tiny hole. Tap the other end with a spoon handle to make a hole about 1/4″ or less across, and pick away the bits of shell. Make sure the hole goes through the membrane. Hold the egg over a dish, large hole down; force the contents out by blowing into the pinhole. Children will enjoy doing this more than you will. Wash out the egg shell by running cold water into the large hole, swishing it around, and blowing it out. When the shells are dry, dye or decorate them. (You can use the egg contents for any recipe not requiring separate whites and yolks.)

Modeling baskets. Using the cornstarch modeling dough recipe given in chapter 3, make a long coil by rolling some dough against a flat surface with the palms of both hands, then coil it around to form the bottom of the basket, and build it up to form the sides. To add new coils, moisten the dough with a bit of water. Press the coils together well so the basket will hold its shape as it dries, and with moist hands smooth the bottom and sides, if desired. Twist two coils together to form a handle. Fasten it to the basket with water after it has dried enough to hold its shape. Or fasten it while still limp and hold it up with a crumpled paper towel. These baskets are particularly pretty if made with lightly tinted dough—pink, pale green, or light blue.

Hanging eggs. An effective but difficult way to hang hollow eggs is to thread a large needle with black thread, tie a very large knot in the end, and thread it through the pinhole from the inside by holding the needle in a pair of tweezers. Look through the egg toward a light to guide the needle through the pinhole.

Or, tie a large knot in the end of a piece of thread, put a dab of glue on the knot, and poke it into the pinhole from the outside, adding another small dot of glue on the outside.

Since small children can seldom tie threads, the best way to fix eggs for them to hang is to use wire. Cut off a 6″ piece of fine wire. Put it in through the pinhole, then out through the large hole, and bend it up on one side to anchor it. Bend the top end of the wire into a hook.

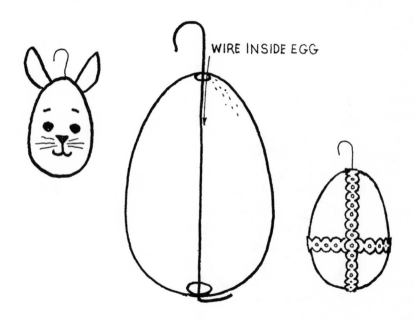

WIRE INSIDE EGG

Easter egg tree. Use a piece of tumbleweed or any attractive branch. If it comes from a living tree, budding may be forced by keeping it in water in the house so that the tree is trimmed with its own buds or leaves as well as the eggs. A dead branch may be painted. Stick the branch in a clay base or wedge it upright in a coffee can using gravel, sand, wadded newspaper and scraps of styrofoam. In addition to hollow eggs, you may decorate the tree with cutouts or paper chains.

Bunny mobile. Use two hangers. Pull one into a circle, and bend the other to form two ears. Leave the hooks intact. Fasten the circle to the ears by tying the hooks together. Tie a big ribbon or crepe paper bow around the hooks. Hang the bunny head by threads attached to the tip of each ear. A good place to put it is in front of a window, hanging from a curtain rod. You can hang hollow eggs at random from this frame, or you can make a face, hanging two for eyes, one for a nose, and, if desired, one for a mouth.

Construction paper baskets. You can use almost any size piece of construction paper but a piece about 6″ × 9″ makes a fairly sturdy small basket. Fold in each of the four sides about 1¹/₂″. Open out the folds. Cut in along each fold line on the short sides to where the fold lines cross (1¹/₂″). Fold the sides up again and glue or staple the ends of the long sides to the short sides. Cut a strip of paper about 9″ long and staple it on to form the handle.
Popsicle stick baskets. You will need about twenty-four Popsicle sticks. If you can't collect that many used ones,

they can be purchased at the five and dime store. Measure the sticks. Most of them are 4$\frac{1}{2}$" long. Cut a square piece of cardboard whose length and width are $\frac{1}{2}$" less than the length of the sticks (usually about 4"). Glue a stick along one edge, and along the opposite edge. Then, putting glue on the ends of these two sticks, fasten two sticks across them on the other two sides of the square. Continue to build the basket up until it is as deep as you would like it. The basket may be painted or shellacked when it is finished. Make a handle from several long pipe cleaners securely twisted together and entwined around the top stick on each side.

Eggshell garden. Prepare the shells by tapping off the top one-third of the egg at the narrow end. After pouring out the egg, tap a small hole in the bottom, and dye, if desired. Use an egg box, painted or not, for a stand, and line each section with a bit of tin foil.

Fill shells with sandy soil, leaving space at the top for watering. Put a few seeds in each and just barely cover with soil. After planting, lay a moist cloth or newspaper over the pots until seeds start to sprout. Transplant to clay pots or garden when plants begin to outgrow pots.

Egg boy. Using an egg shell prepared as described for the eggshell garden, plant grass seed. This will grow and become green hair. Draw a face on the shell and stand it in a collar.

Eggshell pictures. You may want to save the dyed eggshell bits from hardboiled eggs, or simply dye empty egg shells in a variety of colors. These pieces may be glued in a design on construction paper. Or the child may paint a picture and use a few pieces of shell here and there for leaves, rooftops, or sidewalks.

Popcorn lamb or rabbit. Make up a recipe for popcorn balls. Shape the mass of popcorn into a sitting lamb or rabbit. Put it on a paper plate and hold it in place for a minute while the syrup sets. Put it in the refrigerator to harden for an hour or two.

Popcorn picture. Draw the outline of a lamb, rabbit, or chick on a piece of construction paper. Let the child spread the area with glue and fill it in with popcorn. (Set out a bowl of popcorn for eating, too.) You can also fill in the outline with cotton balls.

Cotton ball chicks. On a piece of light colored construction paper, draw a nest or glue on paper grass. For each chick glue two egg shell halves in the nest, and beside them glue two cotton balls to represent a head and body. To complete the chick, draw a small beak and two legs.

Placemats. Outline egg shapes on large sheets of construction paper for the child to cut out and design.

MAY DAY

May baskets. In parts of the United States, the tradition on May 1st is to fill small baskets with grass and candy and leave them by a friend's door. The donor rings the bell, then runs and hides to watch the recipient's surprise. If the donor is spotted, the recipient runs and catches him to kiss him!

Elaborate baskets can be made following the instructions under Easter baskets. Usually, though, May baskets are smaller and are produced in quantity. They may be made from eggshell carton cups, cut apart, painted with tempera; from paper drinking cups, two-, four- or six-ounce size; from soft margarine tubs or small tinfoil pie tins; from paper baking cups or nut cups; from doilies stapled up at four corners; from construction paper, either in the usual rectangular shape or in a boat shape (circle folded in half and stapled together at each end); from squares of aluminum foil molded in muffin tins or pressed into cup shapes in the palm of one's hand, or from small business envelopes, glued shut with the top corners cut out, leaving a handle in the middle.

These baskets may or may not have handles since they usually have to be supported from the bottom anyway. However, children do like handles. Pipe cleaners are easiest, strongest, and good-looking, especially if two are twisted together. Construction paper can be attached to anything. Ribbon, rickrack, bias tape, scraps of material, twisted wrapping paper, braided yarn or crepe paper all make adequate handles. These may be stapled, glued, or tied on.

Fill the baskets with bits of paper grass, if you have some left from Easter, and with candy and cookies, peanuts, small stick pretzels, and other small goodies.

MOTHER'S DAY AND FATHER'S DAY

These holidays are usually celebrated with gifts and cards from the child to the parent, which for small children means a great deal of help and encouragement. In addition to the card and gift ideas given in the following sections, here are two ways of making paper flowers, especially appropriate for Mother's Day.

Tissue flowers. Use three to five ordinary tissue paper handkerchiefs. The prettier the tissues, the prettier the flower. Cut them in half crosswise, open out each half and separate the two layers, piling them as you go. Gather the pile together in your fingers across the middle, lengthwise, and loop a pipe cleaner or other piece of wire around the tissues, twisting it tightly in place. Then carefully pull up and separate each tissue, guiding the petals toward the center to hide the wire and give the flower a rose or peony character. The tips of the petals can be colored with a felt-tipped marker or a bit of water color or tempera.

The same effect can be achieved with gift wrapping

tissue in much more intense colors. Cut it into squares about 4" × 6", or larger or smaller if you prefer. For longer stems, get extra long pipe cleaners, or twist several small ones together, or cut long pieces of wire.

Crepe paper flowers. Starting with an unfolded package of crepe paper, cut a piece off the top about 6" wide. (You can, of course, cut more or less.) This will be across the grain of the paper. While still folded, make a series of small, even cuts along each edge. Unfold. Gather the paper together with your fingers through the middle of the strip. Hook the end of a pipe cleaner or a piece of wire over the gathered middle and twist it tightly. Fluff the flower to fullness. If the wire shows, paste the center petals together over it. These flowers most closely resemble carnations.

HALLOWEEN

Window decorations. Children want traditional decorations: pumpkins, witches, black cats, ghosts, and goblins. You may draw the outlines of these on orange, black, white, and yellow-green construction paper for the children to cut out. (Use white chalk to draw on black paper.)

The child may prefer to construct a witch for your largest window by taping up pieces of black paper which either you or he have cut out: three triangles, two circles, and three strips. One triangle is the hat; under that is a circle for the head, a larger circle for the chest, a triangle for the skirt; the shorter two strips are arms; the longer, narrower strip is a broom handle; and the smallest triangle is the broom.

A four or five year old can make a jack o'lantern from orange construction paper by drawing a circle freehand, or by tracing around a plate, cutting around the circle, drawing eyes, nose, and mouth and cutting them out.

Witch door decoration or hanging. Give the child a sheet of paper for backing; two connected egg carton cups with the long separator between them cut as a unit from the egg carton to form the eyes and nose; a triangle of black paper for the hat; strips of yarn or paper for hair; a few crayons. Show him how to assemble these into a witch's face with hat and hair, and let him glue them on and draw in a mouth, chin, neck, and wrinkles, and color the egg carton eyes.

Paper plate skeleton. Using white paper plates, cut out the following: eyes, nose, and mouth out of one plate for the head; rib structure from a second plate, leaving most of the rim for strength; a rectangle for the pelvis. From white construction paper, cut four arm bones and four leg bones, two hands and two feet. Fasten the skeleton's bones together with string or thread, or use the short, plastic-coated wires that are used to fasten bread bags. These are easily inserted in holes made with a hole puncher. Hang the skeleton where the breeze will move the parts gently.

Jack O'Lantern. Buy a pumpkin. Cut a circle around the stem, making a hole large enough to insert your hand easily. Scrape out the seeds and pulp with a tablespoon. (Save the seeds, separated from the pulp but unwashed, mix them with melted butter and salt and bake them at 250° for 45 minutes to an hour until crisp. A good snack.) Draw features on the pumpkin, using a pencil and keeping the marks light. A five year old will enjoy doing this. He may want to draw ears and eyebrows, or style the face like that of an African ceremonial mask. Using a sharp, pointed knife, cut out the features. This may also be done by the child under close supervision. Fix a candle stub inside by lighting the candle, dripping a puddle of wax on the bottom, and setting the candle in the wax, holding it until it is solid.

Trick or treat sack. A plain brown sack is quite adequate, but children will enjoy making crayon or felt-tip marker pictures, especially in orange and black, of some of the Halloween creatures. Or they may cut pictures from orange and black paper and glue them on.

A much more elaborate affair can be made from a two- or three-pound coffee can. Make a hole near the top at each side by pounding a nail through the can with a hammer. Fasten on a handle—wire, rope, string,or heavy yarn. Paint the can with enamel. Or glue on an orange or black paper cover and decorate it.

Costumes. The child can design his own Halloween costume by crayoning or painting (tempera is very effective) two large sheets of paper that you have cut to his size and stapled together at the shoulders and sides, leaving room for his head and arms. You can get heavy brown or blue wrapping paper from rolls at the packaging desk at large department stores and some hardware stores. Paper dry cleaner bags, especially white ones, do very well.

Crepe paper makes a good costume base because you can choose the color. It can be gathered into a skirt or a cape.

Paper does not adapt well to any sort of pants, for it rips when the wearer sits. Use the child's own trousers, shorts, or tights.

Instead of paper, you may use old sheeting or unbleached muslin for a costume, cut to the size of the child. Be sure to allow space for seams. Double the material, the fold line to lie along the shoulders. Sleeves can be a part of the costume as an extension of the fold line. Be sure to allow enough fullness at the upper arm so that the costume is not binding. Cut a slit for the head about 6″ long and a neck opening about 4″ long. You may bind this with bias tape, leaving the ends on to tie at the neck. Or you may pin the neck. Cut the costume off at the appropriate length. Old materials can be dyed. Or they can be drawn on with felt-tipped markers.

Some costume suggestions: knight, robot, scarecrow, ghost, cartoon characters (Superman, Bugs Bunny), fairy tale characters (Red Riding Hood), favorite story characters (Winnie the Pooh, Raggedy Ann), animals (bear).

Face mask. Cut an oval shape large enough to cover the child's face. Mark center with dot. Slit from chin to center dot, overlap the two edges thus formed, and paste them in place. Cut out eye holes. Color in other features or glue on construction paper features such as a paper cylinder or cone for a nose. Tie the mask on with string or elastic thread, or tape it to a dowel so the child can hold it up to his face. A paper plate can be used in the same way.

Cylinder mask. Cylinder masks are good for a little child who doesn't want his face covered. Form construction paper into a cylinder large enough to fit on a child's head, as for a hat. You may draw features on the cylinder,

such as an animal's face, and glue on ears and nose. Or you may cut overall shapes, such as a bird's profile, in duplicate, and glue one profile to each side of the cylinder, bringing the beaks together in the center of the hat and gluing them to each other.

Paper bag masks. Use a square-bottomed bag large enough to fit easily over the child's head. Cut the top off, far enough down so that the bottom of the bag will sit comfortably on top of the child's head. Slip it on and mark the places where the eye, nose, and mouth holes should be. Take it off and cut out the holes. For very young children, cut out a square or rectangle for the entire face and eyes. Then give it to the child to decorate with crayons or felt-tipped markers, and to glue on construction paper features such as ears, horn, antennae, yarn hair, or beard.

An elaborate robot mask can be made from a paper bag. After cutting it down and marking the eye area, cut out a small rectangle about where the eyes are. Glue a piece of cellophane over this hole. Glue straws on the top for antennae. With a felt-tipped pen or marker, draw on knobs and dials for volume, kilowatt hours, work load.

Hats. Adapt one or more of the party hat suggestions for New Year's to the child's Halloween costume. For example, a paper plate hat makes a bonnet for a pioneer lady costume; a newspaper hat adds the finishing touch to a pirate.

THANKSGIVING

Pine cone turkey. Wind a red pipe cleaner around one end of a pine cone to resemble the neck and head of a turkey, leaving an end hanging down to be the wattles. Wind a black or gold pipe cleaner through the center to form two legs. Add a tail cut from a half circle of colored construction paper and snipped around the edges. The tail can also be made from decorative, colored feathers. Put a drop of glue on the end of each feather and push it down into the cone. You need only four to eight feathers for a very attractive bird.

Apple turkey. Cut a slash around the stem end of an apple. Insert construction paper feathers in the slash. Slash through the blossom and insert a construction paper head on which are drawn the eyes, beak, and wattle. Use three toothpicks so the turkey will stand.

Cone-acopia. Fill an ice cream cone with candy corn or marzipan fruit and lay it on its side as a place favor for a child.

Pilgrim hats. Measure the child's head and cut a hole this size from an $8^1/_2'' \times 11''$ sheet of black construction paper, leaving a tab on the inside of the circle about $3'' \times 2''$. Trim the outside edges so the hat brim is oval in shape. Bend the tab up and, using chalk, draw in the buckle.

Thanksgiving message. Print a short message for the child on heavy paper. For example, "Happy Thanksgiving," "God Gives," or "Thanks to God." The child then glues dried corn on the letters.

CHRISTMAS

Modeling dough tree ornaments can be made in a variety of ways, using the recipe for either the flour or the cornstarch dough given in chapter 3.

Roll out uncolored modeling dough, and cut shapes with table knives and cookie cutters. Mold simple shapes, such as little houses, fish, and birds. Poke a hole through each for a hook. Bake or dry these, paint them (in careful detail or with a single color) with either water colors or tempera, and shellac them.

Mold shapes out of colored dough—small balls, icicles, triangles, diamonds—bake or dry them, squiggle glue on them, and sprinkle them with glitter. Do this over a piece of wax paper so you can pour the excess glitter back into the container.

You may also spray ornaments, painted or unpainted, with gold or silver paint. You may sprinkle damp ornaments with artificial snow.

Styrofoam ornaments can be very elaborate, but even the simplest is very effective on a lighted tree. You need styrofoam balls, any size, a nail, plain pipe cleaners, glue, and glitter. Poke a hole in a ball, twist a loop in a doubled pipe cleaner, cover it with glue, and poke it into the hole. Squiggle glue over half the ball in any design, and sprinkle it with glitter. Do this over wax paper so that the excess glitter can be returned to the container. After this half dries, do the other half of the ball, holding it by the pipe cleaner loop. You can have as many varieties of balls as you have varieties of glitter.

A four or five year old can glue or pin individual sequins to a styrofoam ball. This is very tedious, if one tries to cover the whole ball, so it's best to first put in the loop, then wrap the ball in scraps of shiny wrapping paper, held on with a little glue, and pin in sequins to make a design over the paper. Younger children can just wrap balls in foil wrapping paper.

Cardboard roll ornaments can be made of full length rolls or rolls cut to any size. Wrap the roll with paper such as the foil from cigarette packs. Wrapping paper and tissue paper can also be used very effectively. Glue tiny pieces of any of these over the backing: curled and folded construction paper, Christmas stickers, tiny torn shapes and cut shapes, pieces of plastic cut from margarine tubs, little bunches of nylon net, and pieces of onion bags stretched around the whole thing. Thread a large needle with heavy thread and tie a big knot in the end, run it through the top of the roll and tie it in a big knot on the other side, so that the hook can be fastened on it. Or you may just poke the hook through one edge of the roll and hang it at an angle.

Felt ornaments. Cut hearts, circles, and onion shapes out of double layers of felt, stitch the two layers together, leaving a small opening, stuff them with a little bit of cotton and complete the stitching. Give these to the children to decorate with sequins and glitter. Hang them by slipping a hook through the stitching at the top.

Paper ornaments. Trace a variety of shapes, such as triangles and diamonds, or trace around Christmas cookie cutters on colored paper. Cut these out and decorate them with glitter on designs squiggled with glue. These seem almost too easy, but they look beautiful on a tree.

Yarn dolls also make nice Christmas ornaments, especially if you use varicolored yarn. (For directions see chapter 5.)

Artificial snow. Mix powdered soap with a small amount of water. Beat it until smooth and use it to decorate the tree. Paint it on Christmas cards to give a thick, white look to snowmen, rabbits, or Santa's beard.

Christmas collage. Making a felt banner decoration can be converted to a group activity. Stitch a hem wide enough for a straight curtain rod in one edge of a large piece of felt or burlap. Then collect as many Christmasy items as you can: bright wrapping ribbon, last year's cards, red and green yarn, artificial evergreens and berries, felt scraps, scraps of other materials, several kinds of paper, net, tinsel, pieces of styrofoam, scraps of plastic. If you start collecting a week or two in advance you'll have plenty to work with. Then spread out a lot of newspapers, get out a good supply of glue and scissors, and gather everyone around. Lay out the banner backing, let each one help in cutting, choosing, and placing. Glue everything in place, let it dry, and hang it up.

Centerpiece. Halve a styrofoam ball so it forms a stand, and carve a hole in the top to hold a six-inch candle. Spray paint it and ten toothpicks gold. When it is dry, have the child decorate the base by placing the toothpicks in it and threading a glass bead onto each toothpick. He then winds angel hair around the base and inserts the candle. These are lovely and may be used year after year.

Button calendar. Cut a long narrow strip of green or red felt and sew on twenty-five buttons, one for each day, December 1st until Christmas. Snip a button off daily and when putting away the Christmas ornaments, sew them all back on so you're ready for next year. If that's too much sewing, cut out Christmas shapes such as bells or trees from felt and make a slit in the middle of each so they may be buttoned on and off to mark the days. This device has more meaning to children anxiously awaiting Santa's visit than the usual calendar, because it is tactile.

Reindeer. This door or wall decoration is made from a paper plate. Glue a paper nut cup in the middle for a nose. Cut antlers from construction paper and glue them to the top of the plate. Paint the whole thing brown (unless it's to be Rudolph, in which case paint the nut cup red), and draw on the eyes and mouth.

Milkweed pod poinsettia. Find five milkweed pods, either still lying along the roadsides or resurrected from your fall collections. Paint them red. Glue them in star fashion on a piece of paper with several pieces of evergreen between the pods.

Angel. Make a paper cone 6-8″ high. Glue a Ping-Pong ball or small styrofoam ball on the top of the cone. This will be easier if the cone is open a little at the top. Cut out wings and glue them to the back. You may draw in features on the ball (head) and make yarn hair or you may spray paint the whole thing with silver or gold paint and decorate it with glitter.

Snowman. Have a child cut two circles, one large and one small; two long thin rectangles; and a wide rectangle. He glues the small circle onto the large one and glues the long rectangles, which become arms, to the back of the large circle. These he loops around to the front and staples together. He encases these arms in the wide rectangle by forming it into a cylinder and stapling it. He can then glue on features and a hat.

Christmas tree for the birds. When the holiday is over, remove the ornaments from the tree and place it outside. Put the trunk in a mound of snow, dirt, or sand and tie the top to a clothesline pole or larger tree.

Decorate the birds' tree with long strings of cranberries, which are much easier for little fingers to make than popcorn strings. Use popcorn, too, if you have the patience to help a lot. Tie on balls of sunflower seeds, made by putting seed, millet or dry corn in small containers, poking in a loop of string for a hanger, and pouring in melted paraffin or candlewax. Make more balls by mixing seed or bread crumbs and peanut butter inside wax paper. Stick the balls in the joints of the tree branches; then peel off the paper.

Make pine cone ornaments by filling the openings between the cone's scales with raisins, peanut butter, or gum drops. Hang apple slices by pushing a hairpin or short wire halfway into the slice; tie on by the protruding loop. Tie on chunks of suet, or any fat meat scraps. Put a shallow dish of water under the tree. Scatter horse chestnuts and acorns, left from autumn collecting, under the tree for the squirrels.

If the squirrels are eating all the food so that none is left for the birds, hang the bird food by a long string well away from other branches. Or put food in paper cups and cut a lid of 1/2″ wire mesh just large enough to push down into the cup. Stuff the bottom of the cup with paper to raise the food, fill it with seed, and push in the lid. The birds can get the seed with their beaks, but the squirrels will be frustrated.

GIFTS SMALL CHILDREN CAN MAKE

Children take great pride in making things for others. It is not necessary for the production to be stupendous. In fact, it is very necessary to keep each project within the ability of the child if he is not to feel frustrated rather than pleased with the result. Be a careful judge of what he may be ready to try, and if something is not going well, be willing to drop it rather than press the child to meet a deadline.

In addition to the suggestions which follow, gift ideas can come from other sources. Apple butter and cookies the children have helped prepare, a painting (particularly if mounted), even a song learned for the occasion can be gifts. The important thing to remember is that preschoolers are going to be as interested in the process of making the gift as in the finished product.

Adding the extra to ordinary. The easiest way for a very young child to make a gift is to add his own touch to something else—by pasting pictures, stickers, cloth, cut up paper, yarn, or anything else he can handle to some object. One of the cheapest and most decorative materials is stamps. You may save these or buy a large envelope of them very cheaply at the dime store. Shellac the finished product or coat it with clear nail polish to preserve it.

Any container in the house can be decorated in this way. A cardboard box or a tin bandage box may become a cigarette box. Coffee cans can be pencil holders, crayon boxes, cookie cans, game containers. The center ring of a disposable cellophane tape roll may become a napkin ring. Tin trays, cheap plastic bowls, paper lamp shades may take on new life. Clear or colored glass ashtrays, purchased at the dime store, can be covered on the outside with a decorative layer facing through the glass, and another layer facing out. Or just one carefully chosen picture may be pasted on the outside of the bottom, facing up.

Two year olds can decorate small matchboxes for their fathers and grandfathers by pasting stickers, stamps, or pictures on each side.

Paperweights. Find an interesting large stone, wash it well, and polish it. The child can paint a design on it. Or, just paint it.

If you forget to put the modeling dough away, you may find you've got a lot of paperweights without making any effort at all. Or you can intentionally make paperweights out of the dough, putting a stone in the center of the lump of dough to make it heavier, then shaping the dough and/or texturing it. For a lasting keepsake a child may make his foot or hand imprint in the dough. Very brightly colored dough can be striking, and the youngest child can make a good-looking paperweight successfully.

A more complicated variation is an animal paperweight, made by adding a cornstarch dough head, arms, legs, and tail to a carefully chosen stone. A squirrel, sitting on his hind legs, works well. You may paint this when it is completely dry.

The plaster and vermiculite sculpture described in chapter 3 is quite heavy, and objects made this way have all the characteristics of good paperweights.

Modeling dough jewelry. Buy earring and pin backs (fittings) at the dime store. Using cornstarch dough, mold tiny pieces into attractive shapes, making sure the backs are flat so that they can be glued to the fittings. Larger pieces may be designed as medallions. Be sure to make a hole in these for a string. These pieces may be incised with a large variety of designs. Use a toothpick or a needle for a fine line. Odds and ends make interesting designs: a paper clip makes a petal-shaped impression, a key chain or a light chain can be pressed in to make a checked or plaid design. Coins make overlapping circles, bottle openers make triangles.

Flower petal shapes can be made by pressing bits of dough around one's thumb. Let them dry a bit so that they will retain their shape. Fasten them to a small, flat lump by moistening one end with a few drops of water and pressing them gently together. A piece of dough patted flat and then loosely rolled will make a bud just opening. Pale pink dough in a heart shape makes a Valentine pin.

When thoroughly dry, paint the designs, if desired, with tempera or watercolors. If you use tinted dough, you probably won't want to add paint. Shellac the jewelry or coat it with clear nail polish. Glue to the fittings or thread ribbons through medallions.

Hot plates. Using your rolling pin, roll out a thick (1/2″) slab of cornstarch dough. Cut it into any shape that will make a good-sized hot plate—circle (trace around a saucer), square, flower, apple, leaf—and incise a design in it. Let it dry thoroughly (for several days), paint it if desired, and shellac it.

Decorative stationery. Buy a box of plain stationery or fold typing paper in quarters and buy envelopes to fit. A child may decorate some or all of it in a number of ways. He may paste on a design of cancelled stamps, either as is or cut into interesting shapes. If he is quite young, he may simply paste a decorative sticker in the corner of each sheet. He may print the front page of note paper with a complex potato print design, or he may make just one imprint at the top of each page. He may make a design on each sheet by tracing around a stencil with a colored pencil, crayon, or felt-tipped pen, or by brushing over or spatter painting around a stencil. For other ideas, see the section on greeting cards.

Vases. Paint empty bottles with tempera to convert them to vases. There are now on the market and available at hobby shops and paint supply stores some plastic paints in brilliant colors which make beautiful vases from very ordinary jars. One takes on crystal forms as it dries and hides any painting problems. But you can also cover a jar with papier mache pulp, let it dry, and paint it. You can help a child construct a tall, rather unusual glass structure by gluing several jars on top of each other with epoxy glue. If you top the structure with a very small glass, it may be considered a candle holder. Choose the jars carefully so that the structure is not top heavy.

Handkerchiefs. Use permanent felt-tipped markers or pens to decorate plain men's or ladies' hankies with initials or any interesting, freely made design. Or make a design with crayons and set it by ironing. Let the child experiment first on a rag. Plain bibs may also be decorated this way.

Paper necklace. Cut long, thin triangles from construction paper or wall paper. Cover one side with paste and, starting at the base of the triangle, roll the paper tightly to form beads. Thread the dried beads to make a necklace and shellac it for durability.

Scrubber. Cut a strip of nylon net 6" wide and at least a yard long. Gather it down the middle with your fingers, and wrap it tightly around the middle with fine wire, a pipe cleaner, or a plastic-coated wire twist. Separate the layers of net, making a fluffy ball.

Herb jar. Gather sage and rosemary, preferably in the morning, and pick off the leaves. Dry them in the shade on an old window screen and put them in a gallon container made of tin. When it is full, mix in one tablespoon of salt, close the lid and store it away for a month to cure. (You can also buy boxes of sage and rosemary.) Then decorate a small glass jar with a screw-on lid, fill it, and cap it. By taking off the lid, you will fill a room with a delightful scent.

GREETING CARDS

Children love to get mail and the best way to get some is to send some. They can make a few cards for their own friends, deliver them in person or send them in the mail, and have the pleasure both of making something for someone and of receiving cards in return.

Cards are appropriate for almost all holidays, birthdays, and anniversaries and are almost a necessity as party invitations. Children will want to make a number of cards for Christmas and Valentine's Day. Allow several working periods to make any quantity of cards since a child's interest may flag after doing a few, and don't be surprised if none of his cards looks alike. A child usually will not want to mass produce identical cards but will adapt the original design ever so slightly with each effort or strike out anew each time. This desire is what ultimately stamps the cards as unique, expressing your child's thought and creativity.

Since the size of the envelope determines the size of the card, decide on it first and make the cards accordingly. The small business size envelope (3¹/₂″ × 6¹/₂″) is cheap and convenient. You can, of course, make your own envelopes but this, being a rather boring cutting and gluing task, will generally not interest a child and you will have to do most of it yourself. Such envelopes are made by cutting a piece of paper a little larger than double the size of the card, folding it in half, stapling or gluing it along the sides, and sealing it at the top.

General directions for making cards: Cut the background paper to double the size of the envelope minus a small margin for easy insertion, and fold it in half. Construction paper is heavy enough to take a lot of glue and provides bright color, but typing paper will do. Write a message inside with a felt-tipped pen or a crayon. Many four and five year olds can sign their own names, and three year olds like to pretend they do. Decorate it in one of the following ways or adapt almost any of the painting or paper techniques in chapter 2.

Check the most recent U.S. postal regulations for rules on size, weight, and special problems when making your own envelopes and cards.

Collage. Give the youngest children a supply of old cards, scissors, and glue, or a package of Christmas, animal, birthday stickers, or gummed stars. For more complex effects, get out the collage box (see chapter 2) and use anything even remotely appropriate. Wrapping paper, ribbon, and tinsel are seasonal additions. The child arranges cut and torn bits of anything and everything to his satisfaction, and glues it all in place on the card.

Potato prints are very easy. Use potatoes, cut in half, with a tree or a similar simple design cut into the flat surface. A four or five year old can incise his own design on the cut potato surface with fork, spoon, or table knife by gouging out little pieces. Make a rather thick mixture of tempera and water and brush it on the cut surface. Before printing on the card, make a print on scrap paper to take off excess paint. More complex effects can be made by using two or more designs, overlapping prints, and increasing the number of colors.

Roller prints. Draw a design on a cardboard tube and glue string over the design. Dry it, standing the tube on its end. Paint quickly over the string and roll the tube quickly across the paper.

Stencils. Choose a simple design (bell, ball, tree), cut it out of a piece of heavy cardboard the size of the Christmas card. Show a child how to place it on the card, and brush the open area with paint. Either the outline or the cutout can be used as the stencil. You may buy a can of spray paint made for use on paper, pin the stencil in place over the card with straight pins against a pile of newspaper, and spray. Be sure to cover the adjacent area with newspaper.

Spatter paint by dipping a toothbrush in paint and rubbing it over a piece of screen held about one inch above a piece of paper. Or scrape the toothbrush with your thumb nail, pulling the bristles toward yourself so that the paint splashes away and down on the paper. Practice this with water. Spatter painting is especially effective if it is done in two or more colors.

Before starting to spatter the paper, you may lay a stencil or a variety of objects (bottle cap, paper clip, leaf) on it. When finished, remove the stencil or objects, revealing their shape or design.

Melted crayon. Grate or peel old crayons. The more waxy the crayons, the more beautiful the design. Edible crayons are best of all! Cover the ironing board with newspaper or an old towel, or work on a table protected by a pile of newspapers. Cut a piece of heavy shelf paper, put it on the covered ironing board, spread the crayon flakes on it, put another sheet of shelf paper on top, and iron at very low heat. Obviously a lot of adult help is necessary, but the child can grate the crayons and arrange his design. A five year old can do the ironing with you standing by. Pull the sheets apart, and cut them to the correct size to mount on cards. Use either rubber cement or white glue.

Stamps. Cut stamps into different shapes—petals, leaves, butterflies, birds—or use whole stamps to form a design such as a house. Stamps from other countries are very appropriate for a bon voyage card. Use a Lincoln stamp for Lincoln's Birthday. Cut stamps into small egg shapes for an Easter card. You may get a mosaic effect by cutting the stamps into various forms and fitting them together in a design. Or the stamps, used whole, may be glued on so they overlap for a very complex effect.

Shapes. Cut the card to an appropriate shape. This may be done with one layer of paper to be sent as is. This is the usual custom with valentines. Or the shape may be mounted on a folder of paper. Or a folded paper may be cut into shape in such a way that a hinge is left along one edge: at the top curves of a heart, or at the widest point at one side; at the tassels on a clown's hat, or one hand and one foot; at the top or bottom of a Christmas tree; at the side of a candle holder, or at its bottom.

Movable parts. Use brass paper fasteners to give cards movable parts. For example, fasten a tail which will move to a picture of a dog, or ears that will move to a picture of a bunny.

Or you can make the picture pop out by gluing it to the end of a strip of paper which has been folded back and forth several times, and gluing the other end of the strip to the card. A 2″ piece of pipe cleaner may be coiled around a pencil to make a spring. Glue the bottom coil to the card, top coil to the picture.

Sewing cards. Using very heavy paper or painted cardboard, make your design lightly in pencil. Mark the points where the needle should go through the card. Punch holes at these points with a hole puncher or sharp instrument. You might number them so that the child threads the yarn or embroidery floss through in the correct order. Let him use your largest needle, and a single thread which will be easier to take out if he makes an error. Keep the designs simple: a starburst, with a number of lines of various lengths crossing at the center;

an evergreen tree, with a series of parallel lines of increasing length forming the tree and three short parallel lines forming the trunk. If you plan a design in outline, remember to make two holes at each point so that the yarn outline is all on the top of the card. You may use this technique in combination with others; for example, a nest is sewn on the card with five or six long, criss-crossing stitches. Cotton balls are glued above the nest, and become chicks when legs and beaks are drawn on.

Puzzles. Make a greeting card by drawing or painting a picture and/or a message on a single sheet of fairly stiff paper. Then cut it up in three, four, or five pieces, put it in an envelope, and mail it. Cut straight rather than curved lines.

Valentines. In addition to any technique above (adapted to a Valentine theme by the use of red, white, and pink material), a child may want to work with puns: "Stick with me." (Thread a piece of gum through a paper heart.) "Bee mine." (Draw a bee and a flower and glue candy in the center of the flower.) "My heart shines for you." (Make the heart from red cellophane or foil.) "I've a soft place in my heart for you." (Mount a piece of cotton on a paper heart.) "My heart springs at the thought of you." (Make a coil spring from a pipe cleaner, glue it to the card, and a heart to the other end of the coil.) Hearts in quantity may be made by tracing a cardboard stencil which you have made, or by folding paper in half and cutting a half-heart shape along the fold.

CHAPTER 10

special occasions

Each of the following sections deals with an area which requires extra effort and ingenuity, or some special planning on an adult's part to be successful.

SUCCESSFUL PARTIES

The purposes of a child's party are for the child and his guests to have fun, to celebrate a special occasion, and to bring together children who like each other but may not get to play together frequently. The party is successful if the host and his guests enjoy themselves, and perhaps experience some new adventure together.

Start preparing for a party two weeks in advance in order to maximize its possibilities and provide for your own peace of mind. You can, of course, have a party, especially a tea party, on ten minutes' notice. It is impossible for one adult to run a successful party of more than half a dozen two, three, or four year olds. If you try it, you will probably have to cope with tears, tantrums, and accidents. You can handle more five year olds, but the host may not enjoy himself as much. You may have more guests if several of them are older (six, seven, and eight) and will act as your helpers. A good rule is to have the number of guests equal the child's age. Thus, you would invite two guests to a two year old's party.

Don't forget to ask your child to check the guest list and make suggestions. If you must choose between two equally desirable prospective guests, let the child make the decision. You may run into snags. He may not want to invite a neighborhood child whom you are sure would be very hurt if left out. But this is a good age at which to begin to learn to consider others' feelings.

Decide on the nature of the party. Children like traditional birthday parties—cake and candles, ice cream and balloons, and in fact, regard these as essential ingredients until they are at least six. You will probably want to choose some theme, however, which will help determine the favors, centerpieces, and activities: circus, pirate, fairy tale, any holiday.

When planning the menu for a lunch party or a picnic, remember that, delicious as it may sound to you, and perfect as it may be for a pirate theme, Spanish rice will be practically untouched by your guests. Keep refreshments simple, and choose foods you know the host and his guests really like, such as peanut butter and jelly or chicken salad sandwiches or hamburgers. Serve these with carrot and celery sticks and corn or potato chips, and everyone will eat as much as possible despite the party excitement.

Have an alternate plan ready for a rainy day if your party is planned for outdoors. The most obvious recourse is to move it into the house or the garage. Be prepared with a list of indoor games and activities. If it is at all possible, avoid a postponement. Remember the young child's difficulty in waiting until tomorrow or next week.

Since parties are very likely to bring out the worst in young children, despite their best intentions, be prepared to settle disputes and resolve controversies as quickly, quietly, and painlessly as possible. Some tears are inevitable. Treat them matter of factly and don't let them spoil the party.

If your children are two or three years apart and you want to concentrate on the younger one at his party, you may want to consider arranging for the older one to go visit his Grandma or a very good friend (with a cooperative mother) that afternoon. If he is to stay at home, plan with him just how he can help you—handling the phonograph for musical chairs, demonstrating games, showing little ones how to play with some toys, so that he feels that he, too, is a part of the party despite the lack of activities suitable to his age.

Another possibility that greatly simplifies the entertainment plans is to combine the party with an expedition—to a puppet show, a fire house, a farm, or to the post office to mail letters, written by the children to themselves and addressed by you. Or plan a special (and short) trip on a bus or train. Be sure to arrange these visits in advance with those in charge and, if necessary, make a "dry run" to be sure everything goes smoothly on the Big Day.

If an excursion is your major entertainment, plan to have some travel games during the trip or for passing time before the train or bus pulls out. You will want to work in the ice cream and cake at either the beginning or the end and provide some appropriate favors—absolutely essential at a birthday party. When a child arrives with a present, he will expect to take home something in its place.

Before the party, plan precisely what you are going to be doing for the one to two hours the children will be there. You should have a list of about ten activities, in addition to eating (which will take less than twenty minutes, including blowing out the candles). Avoid competitions for children under six. Preschoolers are neither good winners nor good losers. If you do play pin the tail on the donkey (or the nose on the clown, or the mitten on Santa Claus), either give no prizes, or give each player one piece of candy, and just one extra piece to the winner. Musical chairs is another traditional game for small children which is more fun without prizes and with enough chairs for everyone to have a seat when the music stops. The most successful activities are those in which there is no winner: Simon says, follow the leader, gossip, statues, circle games, marching, singing and acting.

Have a box of rhythm instruments (see chapter 4, Musical Instruments) ready for the children to form a band. You or a child can lead them off, marching all around the house—inside or out—or around the block.

Plan your list of games, alternating active games with quiet ones, and be ready with two or three favorite stories when the children are ready to sit still. This is an especially good idea for the end of the party if the children are to wait at your house for their mothers to pick them up. For suggestions on games, songs, and puppet shows see chapters 4 and 7.

For parties given for two and three year olds only, or if there will be a few very young guests, get out a variety of toys and line them up along the side of the room where the party is to be held. They will prefer to spend most of their time in free play, with perhaps a march around the house before eating, and some singing games, such as "Ring around the Rosy." They also enjoy painting, coloring, and cutting up paper or old magazines, and playing with modeling dough. You may have some four year olds who prefer independent play to group activity. Plan group activities for them, but also provide a variety of toys.

You'll have to decide whether or not you want another adult to assist you. Some two year olds will not want to leave their mothers, in which case you must invite the mother, too.

Some specific suggestions. To plan a party around a theme, decorations are much less important to a young child than making him feel a part of that idea. For example, for a pirate party, provide each child on arrival with a black eye patch and a cutlass. As each child arrives, help him make a pirate hat from a sheet of newspaper. Activities may include marching with pirate flags (black construction paper with chalk skull and crossbones taped to poles of a single sheet of newspaper very tightly rolled), finding buried treasure (a shoebox filled with marbles which will be taken home as favors), and finding hidden pieces of eight (foil-wrapped candy). Hunts may be organized by setting up a succession of clues, or may be simply a matter of everyone looking for what you have hidden earlier.

Making something to take home is an excellent party activity for four and five year olds. Be sure to set out the necessary materials and patterns and provide a demonstration on how something is done—whether it's party hats (see chapter 9, New Year's), masks (see chapter 9, Halloween), or puppets (see chapter 4). Puppet-making can lead to spontaneous shows, another good amusement.

The children may decorate balloons with a felt-tipped pen. Give each child a balloon. Pass around one or more pens. After the children have drawn on the balloons, blow them up. A balloon pump, available at a dime store, is an invaluable aid to a mother short of breath. Or invite some well-known balloon blowers to the party!

WAITING, ANYWHERE

When faced with waiting for an indefinite length of time in the company of small children, you have two alternatives. You may simply expect them to sit still and behave, while you become engrossed in a current magazine. This will seldom happen. It might, perhaps, at the doctor's office, when a sick child is so sick he doesn't feel like doing much else. The other alternative, when you find yourself continually hushing and shushing and reprimanding, is to abandon the magazine and concentrate on the child or children.

If you anticipate a wait somewhere, come prepared with a box of plastic building blocks or a game of pick-up sticks, a coloring book and box of crayons, a toy that has a variety of play possibilities such as a small flannel board, an assembly of plastic parts that can be rebuilt a number of ways, a pair of dice, or a deck of cards. One or two favorite books or a new book from the library may be the best possible distraction. A pad of paper and a pencil makes tic-tac-toe, dot-dash and other pencil games possible, or the child may draw by himself or with help from you. A pair of folding scissors is a real treasure for cutting snowflakes and connected paper dolls. Children also enjoy going through the debris accumulated in a purse, identifying, sorting and counting coins, trading stamps and grocery coupons, and adding them up.

Another way to occupy a child is by playing quiet games. Finger games are especially good during a long church service. Twiddling one's thumbs clockwise or counterclockwise has a long tradition as a quiet busyness and is a challenge to preschoolers. Eensie Weensie

Spider's finger motions are fascinating to a learner, with or without the words. See chapter 7 for more. There are also quiet, although not silent, games like I spy and Dictionary.

If you are taking a child to an evening performance, especially one that will keep him up past his bedtime, a supply of treats in your pocketbook (nonsticky candy, small pretzels, small, uncrumbly cookies) will help revive his energy, as well as give him new interest during especially long or dull (to him) parts of the evening's program.

If you wait routinely at the same place, explore to find the best possible place to wait. You may be able to stay outside, instead of having to sit quietly among adults. There may be a place to run, or treasures to find such as pine cones or violets or nails used in a construction project. A construction project, incidentally, provides hours of spectator joy. There may be a sidewalk for pull toys or small cars or practice in hopping.

If you know you must periodically wait in your car, you may want to keep it stocked. A pile of old magazines in which to search for scrapbook pictures and on which to practice cutting will keep a two or three year old happy for quite a while. Back issues of children's magazines, with their puzzles, stories, jokes and, frequently, pencil and paper activities will fascinate four and five year olds. Keep some blunt scissors and a box of crayons in the glove compartment.

If you must wait an especially long time plan a walk to some specific destination: a library, a dime store or bakery shop, or, best of all, an ice cream and soda shop. Time spent waiting may lead to detailed observation. Decorative murals may have a history, or lead to interesting storytelling. Children may become interested in the identity and function of the great office buildings, department stores and hospitals that surround them, or the history of old houses. The names of streets can lead to speculation, if not knowledge.

TRAVEL

The secret of successful travel with small children is careful preparation and strict adherence to a few rules. When packing your car, allow space for each small child to stretch out to nap. Pack a small blanket for each to keep out drafts or shield them from bright sun. Pack also one special favorite cuddle object—a blanket, stuffed animal, or toy. Plan car activities and pack the necessary equipment. It is a good idea to pack this in a small suitcase with a flat top that can sit crosswise across the back seat to form a work and play table as well as serve as a container.

You may construct a car desk by making a plywood lid for a dishpan. Cut plywood slightly larger than the dishpan. Use four small pieces of wood, about 1" × 1", nailed to the underside of the lid just inside the area of the top edge of the dishpan, to hold the lid firmly in place. You may cut out a circle about 2" in diameter in one corner to serve as a cup holder, making everyone feel more secure when it's time for a drink of water. Cover the lid with a sheet of plastic-coated adhesive paper. Fill the dishpan with toys and snacks.

There is another type of car organizer that takes less space, for it hangs over the back of the front seat, but it provides no work surface. You can improvise one, however, if you include at least one hardbound book or a stiff workbook for a writing surface and have a towel handy that can be spread out on the back seat to make a playing card table.

To make a car organizer, cut out a rectangle of heavy, strong material such as corduroy, sailcloth, or denim.

Cut pockets from the same material or from scraps. Sew the pockets onto the large rectangle. Attach five or six ½" or ¾" twill tapes 40" long to the top and corresponding 6" long tapes to the bottom. The following specifications are for a car organizer about the size of the entire back of the seat. In a two-door car you will need to make two narrower ones and attach one to each seat. You may also want to vary the size of the pockets to fit your own special needs. Cut pockets 1" larger than the desired finished size in both directions.

Cut a rectangle 44" × 19". Hem the raw edges and cut the pockets as follows:

	length		*width*	
one	12"	×	13"	for large workbooks
one	12"	×	11"	for paper supplies
one	12"	×	12"	for books to read
two	8"	×	4"	for scissors and for ruler and pencils
two	7"	×	10"	for small toys and balls and for modeling dough (in a plastic bag)
two	5"	×	9"	for snacks such as raisins, apples (in plastic bags) and cereal
two	6"	×	5"	for box of crayons and for box of playing cards

These dimensions allow a ½" seam allowance for hems at top edges and for turning under on the other three sides. Sew five or six tapes to both top and bottom. If you have trouble getting the tapes between the back and bottom of the seat, open out a wire hanger, then bend the hook a little smaller. Push the hook through from the back to the front of the seat, slide the tape into the hook and pull the hook back through with the tape. You can do

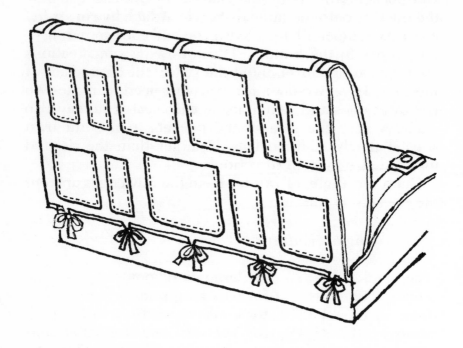

three tapes at a time this way, then slide them into the correct places from the back. Incidentally, a shoe bag, although less efficiently arranged, is a good substitute carrier.

When deciding on books to take along, choose small, lightweight ones if they are to be kept in the pocket much of the time. If you have space in a suitcase, you may pack a few reserve ones and switch them when you stop for the night. For fours and fives, one long book may provide several days' entertainment. Three or four small picture books seem to have the most staying power for two year olds. Two and three year olds especially like to have an old favorite along; it can be invaluable at bedtime in a strange place.

When you are choosing toys to take along, remember to take a very few, very small ones. It is a good idea, especially for two year olds, to avoid toys that can do damage if thrown in a small space. Be sure to include one rubber ball for use during a rest and exercise stop. A few suggestions: plastic building blocks; plastic cars, trucks and construction equipment; plastic animals, astronauts, airplanes, cowboys and Indians; a small wind-up musical toy; a doll and a few doll clothes.

Be sure to pack several pencils and a pencil sharpener, a box of crayons, a stack of cheap paper, including a little colored paper for variety, a small stapler if you have one, some paper clips and rubber bands, a ruler, one or two pairs of blunt scissors, a pack of pipe cleaners, and a deck of playing cards (either a conventional deck which you can sort out for special games or a picture deck which may be adapted to several games).

It is a good idea to invest in one or two new activity books and keep them a surprise for the trip. Sticker fun books and punch-out toys are especially successful. Coloring books and work books add variety.

Modeling dough is a successful car toy. It is compact, easy to store, satisfying to play with, and lends itself to several imaginative games as well as being fun by itself. The free vacuum service offered at so many gas stations takes care of any problem with crumbs.

You will also want a wet washcloth in a plastic bag for a one-day trip, or a supply of foil wrapped, predampened towelettes and a box of tissues. A thermos jar for water will save a lot of drink stops. For little boys a urine jar (any jar with a tight screw top) is a major asset. A thermometer, some bandage strips, a small supply of aspirin (not the kind that can be mistaken for candy), and a tube of ointment or a small spray can of pain killer for brushburns and insect bites are frequently useful.

Plane travel consumes relatively short periods of time and the excitement and novelty of traveling by plane are entertaining in themselves. There is very little space in which to pack toys, so careful choosing is important. Usually the stewardess has a surprise or two in reserve.

Train travel takes longer, but has the great advantage of allowing children to move around much more freely, to get drinks of water and go to the toilet at will. There is also the novelty of the dining car at meal time, and perhaps sleepers or roomettes at night. A small suitcase of toys and activities, and some snacks for between meals, will help while away the hours.

Car travel over a period of several days is the great challenge. With such limited space for movement, and so many hours on the road, the novelty of traveling wears off, no toy is sufficiently entertaining, and you must call up all your inner resources.

You won't want to feel that you act like a social director on an ocean cruise. Expect your children to entertain themselves most of the time. They are most likely to do so if you stop regularly, every hour or two, and get involved in some vigorous exercise—explore a water tower near the road, get a good look at an oil pump, race to the nearest fence and back to the car, get acquainted with some pigs or cows along the roadside or try the swings and slide at a city park. These stops need be only four or five minutes long to be effective. If everybody changes position, either at random or by planned rotation, and takes a different seat on returning to the car, everyone's outlook is improved. Stop early for meals. If children are used to eating lunch at 12:00, start looking for your stopping place at 11:30, and try to have everyone eating by 11:55 at the latest. This bypasses a lot of before-meal crankiness. Eating meals a little early may mean beating the rush hour at roadside restaurants, too. Late afternoon seems to be the worst time for young travelers. If you can possibly do so, stop for the day at 4:00. Here are some games to while away tedious hours.

TRAVEL GAMES

I'm packing my bag. One player starts by saying, "I'm packing my bag to go to_____, and I'm taking a _____." The destination named may be the actual one for the trip, or it may be another, real or ridiculous. You may take things in alphabetical order, so that the first player names something starting with A. The second player adds something starting with B, an alligator and a balloon, for example. Each player is supposed to name everything that has already been packed before adding the item he is going to take along. For two and three year old players, omit the alphabetical order, and don't worry about listing all the other items. They will enjoy thinking up ridiculous things to pack as much as the older children and parents.

Simon says. Play as described in chapter 7, but modify the actions to those that can be done in a moving car. A parent can demonstrate a few to start the game: raise arm straight up, grab your foot, nod your head, shake your head, shake your hand, clap hands, sneeze, stamp your foot, shrug your shoulders.

Add On. Use the same sort of motions described above, and any others that can be managed in a car. One player (usually a parent) starts the game by doing one of these things, and says, "Add on." For example, he or she claps. The next player claps, and at the same time starts to stamp his foot. The third player claps, stamps his foot, and nods his head, everybody continuing all the motions he has started at his turn, adding each of the others as they are introduced, and starting an additional one when his turn comes again. The game stops when no one can do anything else.

Make me laugh. One person says, "Try to make me laugh." He does his best to resist while everyone tries.

The sillier the better. No tickling allowed.

Guessing. Someone (most likely a parent) picks something to be counted. Everyone in the car guesses a number, which is written down by his name. Whatever has been chosen is then counted. The closest guess wins. Anything countable is eligible: letters on a particular coin, crayons or cards in a box, carrot sticks left after lunch, maps in the glove compartment, mosquito bites on the right arm of the youngest child (if he's wearing long sleeves)!

Do you see what I see? The game starts when someone says, "I see something brown," preferably something that the car is just approaching. Everyone guesses: tree, old barn, shed, telephone pole. The correct guesser then takes his turn. If no one guesses right away from the color clue, the first player then gives an additional clue: "I see something with four legs." "Two horns." "Says moo." This game is most successful when the objects are obvious to the guessers, and many objects are guessed in a short time.

Signs. Games using signs are best near towns, and almost impossible on the interstate highways. One child can play alone; two or more may try to beat each other in finding the next letter or number. The children look for the letters of the alphabet on the signs, starting with A, and going through the others in succession. The usual rule is only one letter per sign. Or start looking for one, then two, and so on, either to a predetermined number, or until the children lose interest. Numbers are better than letters in areas with fewer signs because of the availability of route numbers. Parents may play, too, or restrict themselves to refereeing.

License plates. Children just learning their numbers will have fun reading numbers off passing license plates. When four and five year olds are starting to add, they may try adding the last two digits from each plate. Or they may read off the whole plate for a parent to add.

Children also enjoy learning to identify the license plates of different states. If you have a map of the United States, and can spread this out in the back seat, it's exciting to locate the home state of each car and see how far it has come to the spot at which you see it.

How many ways? Circle two cities on the map and have a child trace with a crayon all the possible routes connecting them.

What can you do with? Name any object, such as a single sock, a mitten with holes or a mud ball, and challenge your child to list its many—and fantastic—uses.

Rhyming. One person names an object suggested by the passing scenery (cow, barn), or says any word that comes to mind, and asks for rhymes. The others name as many as they can and come back with words of their own to be rhymed. This leads naturally to nonsense verse.

Counting. Three to five year olds enjoy identifying and counting objects of a certain class: all cars seen for the next two miles; black cars; green signs; telephone poles with one cross bar or poles with two cross bars; high voltage wire carriers. It's especially interesting to pick something unique to the part of the country in which you are traveling: oil pumps in Oklahoma and Texas; cacti in the Southwest; trees with red leaves during autumn in New England; snow patches as you travel north in winter, or into the Rocky Mountains in early summer; tractors as you leave an urban area for the country.

Singing. One of the best times for family singing is in the car during the evening. Let everyone take turns picking songs. Learn the words of your children's favorites; teach them a few of yours. See the list in the Appendix for a few suggestions. In addition, when everyone is feeling silly anyway, make up new words to familiar songs, ("Petunia the Pink-nosed Pricklebush" sung to the tune of "Rudolph the Red-nosed Reindeer"), or turn a play on words into a singsong chant, or sing it to any tune that fits ("How Many Witches in Witchita?").

The continuous story. Someone (usually a parent) starts a story, "Sam Duck made such a big splash whenever he landed on the lake that the fish fled to the bottom and tried to bury themselves in the mud. The other ducks . . . ." Next person's turn. When the story really gets going, everyone will be contributing fast and furiously. Don't worry too much about taking turns in careful succession once well started. Do try to keep each contribution relatively short so that others do not get tired waiting. Keep the subjects within the areas with which children are familiar and make participation easy. Just plain story telling is fun, too!

Pretend packing. A game which children enjoy playing at any time, but especially when the family is looking forward to a trip, is pretend packing. Choose a destination on a map or globe. Decide how you're going to get there: train, plane, ship, car, dog sled. Who will you see there? What will you be doing? What do you need to take? Then get out a paper bag or a small satchel and collect your equipment, real or imaginary. For a trip to the North Pole you may pack a heavy coat, woolen socks, mittens, big boots, vaseline, ice scraper and ice pick, snow shovel, dog toy, candle, matches . . . . For a trip to the South Pacific, include your bathing suit, sun tan lotion, sun burn ointment, umbrella, raincoat, and toy boat.

TRIPS TO LOCAL PLACES OF INTEREST

Small children find the weekly trip to the grocery store an exciting excursion. Think how much more thrilling it is to them to take a special trip. Such trips are adventures, providing much new information and stimulating new ideas and expressions in activities such as painting. A trip may be spontaneous and as simple as asking the gas station attendant to show you around when you drive in for gas at a slow time. Or a trip may be quite involved, requiring careful advance planning to help it go more smoothly.

Certain times of day may be better for your family's excursions. If you have a child who needs an early nap and has difficulty sleeping in a strange place, plan a morning picnic, taking along your lunch, but returning home right after eating it. Or plan a supper trip, to start after nap time. Tired children are not much fun for themselves or for others.

Even if your trip does not include a meal, take along something to eat. Very few children survive happily from breakfast to lunch, or lunch to supper, without a snack. It is also a good idea to have something along to eat if you are likely to face the emergency of being late for a meal. Bring sufficient warm clothing and blankets. Too many are better than too few. Provide a distracting activity for the children during the trip that will help direct the excitement of anticipation on the way there and back.

The best trips are those that seem relatively short to an adult. Even a trip to the zoo, which seems to grownups to be a children's paradise, is best when it is less than two hours long. Children will enjoy museums far more in doses of an hour or less. Furthermore, they will want to move at their own rate of speed, for the most part faster than an adult, but occasionally stopping altogether to study a picture or animal which they find particularly fascinating. When you take children with you to a zoo or museum, move at their rate of speed. If you are going to a museum to study something for yourself, keep it brief or go alone.

Some of the most fascinating trips are to places which adults take very much for granted: bakery, fire house, police station, dairy, farm, or orchard. A very exciting trip for a child is one which takes him to a parent's place of business, particularly if he goes with his parent, or meets him there, and they are able to see or do something on a level which a preschooler can appreciate—even if it is just getting a soft drink from a machine. By familiarizing the child with his parent's occupation, or at least with the place at which it occurs, the occupation and the time spent away from home for that purpose are more acceptable.

Children enjoy exploring large buildings. At a time when it is permissible, go with them through the entire church building, YWCA, library, or office building, or as much of it as is allowed.

For specific points of interest in your community, contact your Chamber of Commerce. Find out where the kindergartens and nursery schools take their classes on field trips, and get a map pinpointing the different parks in your community. To a child each playground has its own personality, so don't frequent only the one closest to home.

When you're at a park take time to play "silence" by having your child sit quietly with his eyes shut and try to identify what he hears. Or play "bring it back" by having your child find something such as a leaf, bring it to you, and then be sent off for the next item. With a list of five items, one being a piece of litter, you'll have made your child happy and the park a bit prettier.

A SPECIAL TIME AND A SPECIAL PERSON

When parents work, the evening hours assume extreme

importance in establishing firm family bonds. How tempting it is for parents to prop their feet up and open the newspaper or water the lawn or sort a load of wash, despite the fact that the children seem intent on bringing the roof down. Both parents are tired, have demanding household tasks, and are almost as hungry as the children. The solution consists in careful planning.

The working mother may need extra help to see that chores are done—perhaps more family cooperation, perhaps outside help, such as a teenage babysitter to free her for an hour of furious cleaning. She may have to content herself—as most mothers must eventually—to the fact that the house can stand neglect, but children can't.

Planning must also go into scheduling meals. How quickly can the little ones be fed? Should the parents' meal be delayed until the children are in bed?

When making the supper menus out, Mother can jot down ideas for a daily "children's hour." The ideas should be something everyone enjoys doing together. By exploring different chapters in this book, parents will find many suggestions and may develop new interests themselves. Painting need not be a feminine activity and football a masculine one. Little boys are anxious to express themselves in paint and drawing but will quickly "wise up" if Daddy consistently sits on the sidelines. Similarly there is no reason why Mother and daughter cannot learn to pass, punt, and kick. Flag football (in which a "tackle" consists of pulling a protruding hankie from the ball carrier's pocket) is ideal for families.

Even in a family where the Mother works at home, evenings should be just as carefully planned. Although a man may dearly love his children and look forward eagerly to seeing them each evening, he may not necessarily know what to do with them once he's seen them. He is at his least inventive at 6:00 p.m., yet the children clamor for his continued attention. Roughhousing is the most spontaneous solution, and in fact, one of the best, but it's a good idea to have a few other suggestions on tap.

Reading and telling stories is ideal. Parents' stories can be very exciting, adventurous or spooky, and tales of their childhood create a special bond. Quiet games such as tic-tac-toe, pick-up sticks and word games are short, good preludes to bedtime. Card and board games are somewhat longer, but may be engrossing to parent as well as child. More inventive are shadow play, puppet shows (put on with the parents as well as for them), pantomime, riddles, and magic tricks. Fathers are frequently very good at sleight-of-hand, at least in the eyes of their two to five year old children. Family singing is a particularly good bedtime activity. A variation is acting out songs on records. Marching and dancing are extra special when done with one's parents. (For specific directions for each of these activities, see chapters 4 and 7). A slightly longer block of time will allow for some experiments, or the construction of a robot costume from paper bags, or a fort from cushions, blankets, and boxes.

Try starting a large project, such as building a fort or digging a big hole, which the children can work on alone and on which father and children can work together for a few minutes every day or two. Do a little planning, gather essential materials, anticipate the children's limits and work around them. Father can construct the framework for the fort; the children can nail on the board siding. Or Father can straighten the sides of the hole and loosen dirt for the children to remove. A garden is one of the most rewarding of such projects.

Father and child can map a few city blocks, walking along different streets each evening, observing size and position of buildings and alleys, noting them roughly, and on their return home doing a detailed drawing. In midwinter they can map the basement or attic together, child holding tape measure and flashlight. This is a very good activity for the three to five year old who has nameless fears of a dark basement, and may even lead to plans for using the space. Fathers may also get involved in elaborate constructions with plastic block sets, mechanical building sets, toy railroads, and car racing tracks. Here a man must be careful to share his ideas, talk about what he is doing, and let the child really join in the work rather than get in his hair.

On weekends most working men and women get to spend larger amounts of really productive time with the children. Routine tasks such as cooking, cleaning, shopping, car washing, lawnmowing, garden care and fix-it jobs are also opportunities for companionship. If a man is going to enjoy a child's help, however, he must recognize that this help will probably make the job take a little longer; that he must set the child's task within specific limitations of attention span and ability; and that he must keep his expectations within reason, and call upon his reserves of patience if necessary. For example, washing one wheel of the car is a big job for a three year old, whereas a five year old might he expected to do all four. Any child will want to run errands when asked, but if he's to get the hammer, the hammer must be where he can find it. A job is more pleasurable if done with someone, for a child will enjoy raking alongside his father far more than he will enjoy the task of raking one section of lawn alone. A child doing a job with which he is not familiar will need careful, detailed instructions from his parent, who must try to see the task from the little one's point of view in order to describe its requirements accurately.

When a child is unable to actually help in a job, he will still enjoy being near his father doing something similar to what his father is doing. For example, Mother and children can play Fox and Geese in the grass in random paths mowed through it by Daddy before he starts his serious mowing. (See directions in chapter 8, Winter.) Or a child may hammer his nails into his piece of wood while his father is busy building or repairing.

Find a way for the child to enter into the spirit of the building, gardening, sailing, cooking, music or whatever fascinates most. A very special treat for a child is riding along with his father when he has to make a quick trip to his place of work. And there is the whole world of sports. A set of plastic football or baseball players and a marked-off poster board in the general vicinity of his father will let a child feel something of a participant in the Saturday afternoon games on television. From the age of one on, a game of catch is a good excuse for a few minutes of fresh air. Attitudes about fair play and good sportsmanship are transmitted along with the ball. Don't forget kite-flying, hurdle-jumping (the mud hole can become a sawdust pit), soccer, foot racing (with father severely handicapped, of course), and paper boat launching.

Make up an expedition to find a short cut to the nearby railroad track or candy store, or to locate a blue spruce or the first tulip. Pack a paper bag with an apple and cookie for each member. Hike rather than walk. (This is where you need a back pack to tote a child under two.) Keep it short, for there's no need to set endurance records. And do it often!

Throughout their first years young children favor one or another parent at different times. At two and a half a girl may shrink from her father, but in a few months he will be her dearest friend. At five a boy will idolize the men in his life, much to the consternation of his female kindergarten teacher. How necessary it is that children be provided with solid male/female companionship when they are little!

For many reasons, parents often find little time to play

with their children. A father may be moonlighting at a second job, both parents may still be students, the mother may work outside the home or she may find the household routine too demanding in itself to allow time for playing. But the work of a child is play and he needs help to do it well, to develop in a way his parents envision.

ENTERTAINING THE SICK CHILD

A very sick child wants cuddling and cosseting, but is not usually demanding until he begins to recover. The not very sick child, too unwell to play outside but not sick enough to stay in bed, cranky because he is unaccustomed to feeling bad, and discontented because he is bored, is a major challenge to an adult's imagination. Even though he need not necessarily stay in bed, he is not ready to play actively, and he is very dependent on you for his entertainment.

In our electronic age, we have major aids. Television viewing (don't forget the educational channels), a radio for the child to tune himself, and a phonograph with his favorite records may give you time to wash the dishes and do the laundry. A young child will not be satisfied to be a passive listener indefinitely, however. Be ready with suggestions for specific tasks, unless the child is practically well. While ill, he won't feel up to much creative thinking. For example, present selected materials from your collage box, with a specific suggestion for their use. The child may do something else with the materials, and may ask for more to fit his idea, but he won't have to face the task of creating order out of a large number of choices.

It is a useful rule to remember to select those games, crafts, and activities which are somewhat easier than his favorites when he is well. The games he enjoyed six months or a year earlier, involving no difficult learning and little or no frustration, are good choices.

A particularly good activity for a sick child is looking through family photograph albums or his baby book. If you sit with him and tell him the stories of the pictures, or explain the significance of the keepsakes, he will be fascinated. Children particularly like pictures of themselves as babies and pictures of their parents and grandparents as children.

Similarly if your child has a special interest such as cars or dolls, he may make a scrapbook, especially if you have old catalogs on hand or have obtained leaflets on these in anticipation of a confinement.

If the child is so sick that he must stay in bed, arrange to do some chores in his room to keep him company. For a long convalescence you might arrange a day bed near the rest of the family on a couch or cot, moving him back to his own room for quiet times, naps, and bedtime. This may be the time to bring out toys that have been packed away because they've lost their appeal, they're for younger children, or they're broken. He may be able to sort out a kitchen drawer or scrape carrots. If you have a bird, fish, or turtle, place it where your child can observe it from his bed.

Usually you and he will feel better if you keep his room neat and attractive, organizing all the necessary paraphernalia so that he can start and complete a task without being dependent on you. In a box or can collect scissors, crayons, pencils, pencil sharpener, felt-tipped markers, hole puncher, stapler, and glue. Provide a stack of various paper: construction, plain white, lined, newsprint, and tissue paper; a coloring book or two, an activity book, some old magazines; and an old newspaper or oil cloth he can work on. And, of course, he must have at hand the necessities: a box of tissues, glass of water (a small pitcherful if you are pushing fluids), and paper bag or small wastebasket. For real convenience, you can pin the paper bag by its turned-down edge to the sheet.

Give a bedridden child a bell he can use for calling you, and work out a system whereby he can ring a little and gently for general attention, loud and hard for emergencies. Provide him with a bed-desk, perhaps one as simple as a cardboard carton with two rectangles cut out of opposite sides to provide leg space. Or hunt up the dishpan desk used when traveling and stock it. Put a couch cushion behind his back or let him sit on it to vary his position.

Designate a wall area within his vision for hanging pictures—his choice or his own work. If you are worried about the wallpaper or paint, fasten a bright ribbon from corner to corner and pin papers to that. If a child is in bed over a holiday, even a minor one, observe it with considerable fuss: decorate his room, put on his best pajamas (green for St. Patrick's Day), put a favor on his tray, and try to adapt his food to the occasion. He may feel well enough to make favors or place cards for the whole family, but if he bogs down in the middle, help him finish quickly so he is not burdened by the task.

The days are terribly long for a child confined to bed. You want to vary his existence without overtiring him. A three-minute alcohol rub is stimulating, as is periodic face washing and hair combing. His clock-watching can be directed toward helping him tell time. You can set an alarm clock for different times—lunch, cartoons, medicine doses—and talk about the meaning of the numbers. To break up the day, give meals a flair. Having a meal in bed can be a special treat if the tray has an attractive placemat cut in an animal shape from a wallpaper sample, a straw in a glass, crusts trimmed from the bread and so on. Dig out leftover special occasion napkins for a touch of color and fun. Plan regular snacks as well as meals and lure a reluctant appetite with a bit of novelty: core an apple and slice it crosswise; cut an orange into four or six different-shaped pieces; put ice cream and food coloring in an egg nog for a pink egg shake.

Visitors are wonderful, but sometimes terribly tiring. Don't let children or adults gather in the sick room. One adult at a time, who will chat with the patient, play a quiet game or two, or read or tell a story, is invaluable. If several guests arrive at once, let everyone quickly say hello, then move all but one into another room with you and arrange for taking turns. If your child's visitors are his age, structure the activity—suggest a specific game or play activity such as small cars or paper dolls. A sick youngster will be fatigued quickly by a healthy one and will truly enjoy only the shortest visits. Brothers and sisters, if they can adapt to the sick child's level of activity, are a major asset, but for their own sakes as well as his, don't let them settle in to stay for hours. The little toys, games, treats and sweets brought by visitors are marvelous, but remind your nearest relatives of the existence of other children in the family if they are being overlooked too frequently by guests. The mailman's arrival is a bonus when he is carrying get-well cards. A parent's homecoming is apt to be the biggest event of the day, and if he should happen to have a candy bar or two with him for dessert, that day is special.

If you are giving three or more medicines four or more times a day and taking routine temperatures, make a chart for yourself so you can simply check off and write in. Leave a space beside each dosage time and note anything unusual or interesting enough to report to the doctor. Put liquid medicines in tiny glasses or tube-shaped medicine dispensers and let the child serve himself as soon as he is old enough to handle a cup. If a medicine is particularly unpleasant, give him a strong-flavored drink first, like orange juice, and help him get the medicine down while the tastes buds are numb. Have water or juice handy to follow the dose immediately. Be absolutely firm with each dose, and even a one year old will stop raising objections within three days. And don't hesitate to ask another adult to dispense the medicine for a day or two, or just give an occasional dose, if you find you are engaged in a battle of wills.

When it is time to return to a full existence after a long illness, a child may be very reluctant. He has adapted to his confined existence, and as much as he may want to get back to normal, each step forward requires great effort. His energy level is low and he is used to being cosseted. Discuss in detail his return to preschool or kindergarten. Talk about his teacher and friends, (he may have trouble remembering their names!), the activities, the learning. Help him choose things to take for show and tell. Set the day for his return several days in advance, letting him help decide exactly which day— and consider that a week starting on Wednesday or Thursday is a nice short one. Let him plan his getting up, dressing, eating, and leaving the house. Will he walk or ride? Who drives the car pool that day? Who will be on the school bus? Help him recall what happens on arrival—free play or opening exercises. What toys can he look forward to using? Sing school songs, play school games, and, in fact, play school! If he is coming home exhausted and you fear a setback, consider arranging for a temporarily shortened school day.

When a small friend or neighbor is the patient, both recipient and donor will benefit from assembling a get-well box. With the child donor's help, fill a box with a variety of items—a paper airplane, a homemade puzzle, an envelope of grass seed to be "planted" on a wet sponge. Crown the box with a get-well card—an original creation, of course.

list of materials

THINGS YOU MAY ALREADY HAVE OR WILL WANT TO SAVE

Pieces of cord
Styrofoam sheeting
Rope
Shells
Rings: canning, embroidery hoops
Scraps of tarpaper, vinyl, linoleum
Old blankets
Egg shells
Empty spools
Onion bags
Used wrapping paper
Cardboard tubes
Burst balloons
Clothespins
Scraps of cloth, ribbon, yarn, threads, trims, felt
Pieces of broken toys
Small jingle bells
Nut shells
Empty food packages and cans
Old toothbrush
Old pieces of screening
Wax paper
Rocks and stones
Walnut shells
Tongue depressors or Popsicle sticks

Cardboard cartons
Pieces of cardboard: light, heavy, corrugated
Candle stubs
Blunt knife
Tweezers
Interesting branches
Coat hangers
Tin foil
Paper grass
Facial tissue
Cookie cutters
Rolling pin
Fingernail polish, clear
Hair spray
Straight pins
Safety pins
Paper cups, regular and cone shapes
Buttons
Wallpaper samples
Empty bandage boxes
Interesting bottles
Old medicine bottles
Jars: all kinds, but especially baby food jars
Small business envelopes ($3^{1}/_{2}'' \times 6^{1}/_{2}''$)
Old greeting cards
Bottle caps

Pop top tabs
Empty plastic detergent and bleach bottles
Empty milk cartons
Acorns, leaves, chestnuts, pine cones, seed pods
Stamps (canceled, mailing, and advertising)
Bags, all sizes
Old magazines
Old sheeting
String, variety of thicknesses
Toothpicks: round and flat
Straws: plastic and paper
Cotton
Paper plates: dessert and dinner size
Small pad of paper
Pencils
Dishpan
Wood scraps
Nails, large
Scraps of plastic-coated adhesive paper
Twill tape
Snaps
Hooks and eyes
Pencil sharpener: large and pocket sizes
Ruler
Shoe laces
Rubber bands
Wooden matches
Laundry bleach
Moth balls

Hydrogen peroxide
Bits of brick
Oatmeal boxes
Shaving cream
Comb
Pastry brush
Foil pie pans
Cigar box
Old clothes: hats, shoes, socks, gloves, mittens
Empty soda bottles
Old newspapers
Egg boxes
Large box for collecting miscellaneous scraps
Flour
Salt
Cornstarch
Soap flakes
Baking soda
Baking powder
Vinegar
Food coloring
Detergent: liquid and dry
Liquid laundry starch
Powdered cleanser
Feathers
Salad oil
Wooden spatula
Sand
Petroleum jelly
Pliable plastic: coffee can lids, margarine tubs
Hammer
Nylon net

THINGS YOU WILL WANT TO BUY NOW

Dry tempera: primary colors (red, blue, yellow), black and white

Large artist brushes

Crayons: edible for younger children

Felt-tipped pens and markers: several washable and one permanent

Newsprint, plain and colored (12″ × 18″)

Blunt scissors: right or left handed

White glue

Colored construction paper (12″ × 18″)

Colored and white chalk

Cellophane tape

Typing paper

Pipe cleaners: white and colored

Balloons

Heavy shelf paper

Thread: Size 8 black, buttonhole

Wire: 18-gauge galvanized (available at hardware stores)

Styrofoam balls in a variety of sizes

Ruler

Household cement

Roll of large brown paper

Playing cards

THINGS YOU MAY WANT TO BUY LATER

Water colors

Carbon paper

Rubber cement

Tissue paper, colored

Crepe paper

Clay (10 lb. bag)

Sawdust

Plaster of paris (10 lb. bag)

Wire for sculpturing and tying

Liquid plastic

Vermiculite (available at nurseries)

Plasticene

Metal and wooden dowels

Onion skin paper

Brass paper fasteners

Spray paint: gold and silver

Shellac

Litmus paper (available at drug store)

Pieces of oilcloth to cover table

Glitter

Alum (available at drug store or spice shelf of gro-

cery store)
Glycerine (available at drug store)
Hole punch
Stapler
Balloon pump
Child-size sponge mop
Blotting paper
Kitchen timer

Hand mirror and floor length mirror
Thermometer and barometer
Large magnet
Magnifying glass
Compass
Notebooks: large and small

songs for group singing

Aba Daba Honeymoon

Alouette

The Bear Went over the Mountain

Bye Baby Bunting

Carolina Moon

Clementine

Danny Boy

Dixie

Down in the Valley

Erie Canal

Farmer in the Dell

Give a Little Whistle

Glow Worm

Good Morning, Mary Sunshine

Go Tell Aunt Rhody

Harvest Moon

He's Got the Whole World in His Hands

An Irish Lullaby

Jacob's Ladder

Jimmy Crack Corn

Jingle Bells

John Henry

This Land is Your Land

Lavender Blue

Mairzy Doats

Merrily We Roll Along

Michael, Row the Boat Ashore

Mr. Moon

Oats, Peas, Beans, and Barley Grow

Oh, Christmas Tree

Oh, How Lovely Is the Evening

Old Man River

One More River

Onward, Christian Soldiers

Polly Wolly Doodle

Puff the Magic Dragon

Reuben, Reuben

Rock Island Line

Rudolph, the Red-nosed Reindeer

She'll Be Coming Around the Mountain

Shortenin' Bread

Swing Low, Sweet Chariot

Sur le Pont d'Avignon

They Built the Ship Titanic

The Watermelon Rind

We Wish You a Merry Christmas

When Johnny Comes Marching Home

When the Saints Go Marching In

When You Wore a Tulip

Yankee Doodle

Zippidee Doo Dah

BIBLIOGRAPHY

Adair, Margaret Weeks. *Do-it-in-a-day Puppets for Beginners.* New York, John Day Co., 1964.

Beck, Joan. *How to Raise a Brighter Child; the Case for Early Learning.* New York: Trident Press, 1967.

Bettelheim, Bruno. *Dialogue with Mothers.* New York: Free Press (Macmillan), 1962.

Boni, Margaret Bradford (ed.). *Fireside Book of Folk Songs.* New York: Simon and Schuster, 1947.

Chirel, Kinneret. *The Complete Book of Hanukkah.* New York: Friendly House Publishers, 1959.

Chukovsky, Kornei. *From Two to Five.* Berkeley and Los Angeles: U. of Calif. Press, 1968.

Collin, Lore. *Stampcraft.* Charles Tuttle Co., 1960.

Dairs, Barbara. *Learning Science through Cooking.* New York: Sterling Publishing Co., 1963.

Feingold, Abraham. *Teaching Arithmetic to Young Children.* New York: The John Day Co., 1965.

Fletcher, Helen Jill. *The Big Book of Things to Do and Make.* New York: Random House, 1961.

Follett, R. J. R. *Your Wonderful Body.* Chicago: Follet Publishing Co., 1961.

Fraiberg, Selma H. *The Magic Years.* New York: Scribner, 1959.

Frankel, Lillian and Godfrey. *101 Best Action Games for Boys.* New York: Sterling Publishing Co., Inc., 1968.

Grollman, Earl A. (ed.). *Explaining Death to Children.* Boston: Beacon Press, 1967.

Gilbert, Arthur and Oscar Tarcor. *Your Neighbor Celebrates.* New York: Friendly House Publishers, 1957.

Hainstock, Elizabeth G. *Teaching Montessori in the Home.* New York: Random House, 1968.

Hamsher, Florence. *The Complete Book of Children's Parties.* Garden City, New York: Dolphin Books, 1949.

Ilg, Frances L. and Louise B. Ames. *Child Behavior.* New York: Harper and Row, 1955.

Ilg, Frances L., Louise B. Ames, Evelyn Goodenough, and Irene Andresen. *The Gesell Institute Party Book.* New York: Harper Bros., 1956. [Paperback: Dell, 1963]

Jafee, Leonard. *The Pitzel Holiday Book.* New York: Ktan Publishing House, Inc., 1962.

Kellogg, Rhoda. *The Psychology of Children's Art.* [A *Psychology Today* Book.] New York: Random House, 1967.

Krauss, Ruth. *How to Make an Earthquake.* New York: Harper and Bros., 1954.

Lewis, Shari. *Folding Paper.* New York: Stein and Day, 1963.

Meilach, Dona Z. *A Doctor Talks to 5-8 Year Olds.* Chicago: Budlong Press Co., 1966. (available through doctors)

Nelson, Glenn C. *Ceramics.* New York: Holt, Rinehart and Winston, 1960.

Newson, David (ed.). *190 Children's Songs.* New York: Robbins Music Corp., 1967.

Pines, Maya. *Revolution in Learning.* New York: Harper and Row, 1966.

Sanders, Herbert H. *Pottery and Ceramic Sculpture.* Menlo Park, Calif.: Lane Books, 1964.

Saunders, John R. *The Golden Book of Nature Crafts.* New York: Golden Press, 1958.

Schegger, T. M. *Make Your Own Mobiles.* New York: Sterling Publishing Co., 1965.

Schneider, Herman and Nina. *How Your Body Works.* New York: William R. Scott, Inc., n.d.

Schwartz, Alvin. *The Rainy Day Book.* New York: Trident Press, 1968.

Skelsey, Alice. *The Working Mother's Guide to Her Home, Her Family, and Herself.* New York: Random House, 1970.

Teaching Johnny to Swim. Washington, D.C.: The American Red Cross, 1963.

Wensberg, Katherine. *Experiences with Living Things.* Boston: Beacon Press, 1966.

Whitman Creative Art Books. Racine, Wis.: Whitman Publishing Co., 1966.

Winn, Marie and M.A. Parker. *The Playgroup Book.* New York: Macmillan, 1967.

FOR LISTS OF RECOMMENDED READINGS, WRITE TO:

Public Affairs Pamphlets, 381 Park Ave., S., New York, N. Y. 10016.

Child Study Association of America, 9 E. 89th St., New York, N.Y. 10028.

Superintendent of Documents, U.S. Government Printing Office, Washington, D. C. 20402. (Indicate your area of interest.)

National Recreation Association, 8 W. 8th St., New York, N. Y. 10004. (Enclose payment of $1.50.)

index

Building, boots, 66; forts, 174, 228; rubberband board, 109
Buildings, paper cutout, 106
Bunks, 174
Bunny mobile, 186
Butterflies, 169; net for, 169
"Button, button," 148
Button calendar, 198
Button-up bear, 99
Buttons, in pictures, 41; in plaster plaques, 63

Camping, at home, 175; rainy day, 175
Can, for percussion instrument, 85; for telephone, 99; for trick or treat, 192; used as baby toy, 21
Candle holder, from jars, 203; modeling dough, 50
Candles, experiments with, 114; wax resist, painting with, 37
Car, desk for, 216; organizer, 216–218; waiting in, 215
Carbon dioxide, 116
Carbon paper, use of, 29
Cardboard, detergent pictures on, 38; hats, 182; pictures, 41; puppet, 92
Cardboard carton (See Carton)
Cardboard roll, instrument, 85; ornaments, 196;puppet, 91; stethoscope, 107
Cardholder, 132
Cards, greeting, 204–208; planning of, 177
Card games (See Games, card)
Carnations, colored, 121; paper, 189–190
Carrot tops, growing of, 122
Carton, for baby, 22; for doll house, 104; for play house, 105; for puppet theatre, 91; for refrigerator, 49; for stove, 49
Castle tower, oatmeal box, 107
"Cat and mouse," 150
Catch, playing, 21, 230
Caterpillars, 168
Cellophane, butterflies, 72; looking through, 98; in toothpick structures, 72; on windows, 38; pictures, 41
Cereal (See Dry cereal)
Chains, paper, 44, 106
Chalk, coloring sand with, 40; on side-

walk, 176; on wet sheeting, 37; painting with, 37; stenciling with, 32
Chemistry, 113
Chimes, 85
Christmas, 180, 195–200; angel, 198; button calendar, 198; centerpiece, 198; collage, 197; mobile, 70; poinsettia, 198; snowman, 199
"Christmas Is Coming," 84
Christmas tree, for birds, 199; ornaments (See Ornaments)
Cigar box guitar, 86
Clay, 52; building with, 56, 57; drying, 53; firing, 54; forming of, 129; glazing, 55; leaf impressions, 156; sawdust, 62; texturing, 54
Cleansing powder, painting with, 38
Clock, cardboard, 109
Cloth book, 96 (See also Texturebook)
Clothes hanger (See Wire hanger)
Clothing, and temperature, 125; in winter, 157
Clouds, 126
Clover chains, 170
Clown puppet, 92
Coat hanger, wire (See Wire hanger)
Coil, animal, 58; clay, 56; modeling dough, 51
Collage, 38; box, 28; Christmas, 197; for sick child, 231; greeting cards, 205; scrap paper, 38; sticker, 39; techniques, 28; tissue paper, 39
Collecting, butterflies, 169; leaves, 154; rocks, 129; stamps, 130
Color cards, 141
Coloring eggs, 183
Columbus Day, 180
Compass, 125, 127
Competition, in games, 131, 211
"Concentration," 132
Condensation, 115
Cone-acopia, 195
Confetti, in painting, 36
Constellations, 126
Construction paper scraps, 36
Continuous story, 224
Convalescence, 235
Cooking, 113
"Cootie," 146
Cosmic mobile, 70
Costumes, 192–193